SURVIVAL CHINESE

How to Communicate
Without Fuss or Fear—Instantly!

by Boyé Lafayette De Mente

TUTTLE PUBLISHING
Tokyo • Rutland, Vermont • Singapore

Published by Tuttle Publishing, an imprint of Periplus Editions (HK) Ltd., with editorial offices at 364 Innovation Drive, North Clarendon, VT 05759 and 130 Joo Seng Road #06-01/03, Singapore 368357.

LCC Card No. 2005297344
ISBN 0-8048-3605-1

Printed in Singapore

Distributed by:

Japan
Tuttle Publishing, Yaekari Building 3F
5-4-12 Osaki, Shinagawa-ku
Tokyo 141-0032, Japan
Tel: (03) 5437 0171; Fax: (03) 5437 0755
Email: tuttle-sales@gol.com

North America, Latin America & Europe
Tuttle Publishing, 364 Innovation Drive
North Clarendon, VT 05759-9436, USA
Tel: (802) 773 8930; Fax: (802) 773 6993
Email: info@tuttlepublishing.com
www.tuttlepublishing.com

Asia Pacific
Berkeley Books Pte Ltd
130 Joo Seng Road, 06-01/03
Singapore 368357
Tel: (65) 6280 1330; Fax: (65) 6280 6290
Email: inquiries@periplus.com.sg
www.periplus.com

08 07 06
8 7 6 5 4 3

TUTTLE PUBLISHING® is a registered trademark of Tuttle Publishing.

OTHER BOOKS BY THE AUTHOR

Instant Japanese
Japan's Cultural Code Words
Chinese in Plain English
Japanese for the Travel Industry
China's Cultural Code Words
Japan Encyclopedia
Mexican Cultural Code Words
Mexican Etiquette & Ethics-
Anticipating & Understanding Mexican Social & Business
   Behavior
Japan's Business Code Words
Korea's Business & Cultural Code Words
Cultural Code Words of the Hopi People (e-book)
Cultural Code Words of the Navajo People (e-book)
Nihon Rashisa wo Eigo ni Dekimasu Ka (with Michihiro
   Matsumoto)
Naze no Ei-Tango 230 (Loaded English)
Tsuji-nai Katakana Eigo-Meanings & Uses of Japanized English
   Words (with Michihiro Matsumoto)
KATA-The Key to Understanding & Dealing With the Japanese
Instant Chinese
Instant Korean (forthcoming)
Survival Chinese (forthcoming)
Survival Korean (forthcoming)
Tokyo Subway Guide: Hundreds of Key Destinations
   (forthcoming)

Contents

PREFACE

The "Language Wall" is Down!

There are at least eight primary Chinese languages, and although they belong to the same family and historically have been referred to as dialects, they are as different as French, Italian, Spanish and other so-called Romance languages, if not more so.

Westerners have also traditionally regarded learning and speaking any of the Chinese "dialects" as especially difficult because they are all "tonal languages." That is, changing the tone of voice in the pronunciation of words changes the meanings of the words.

These circumstances, combined with the forbidding appearance of the "characters," or ideograms, used to write all of the Chinese languages, have long been viewed by Westerners as insurmountable barriers. Furthermore, many Chinese words have dozens to over a hundred homonyms [words that are spelled the same and may be pronounced the same but have different meanings], further complicating matters.

The National Language

But this view of the Chinese language is outdated. In 1949 the newly established Communist government of Mao Ze-dong decreed that Mandarin Chinese, the "dialect" spoken in Beijing and the surrounding areas, was to be the official language of China, and thereafter would be taught in all of the schools throughout the country.

Today, virtually all Chinese speak Mandarin Chinese, known as ***putonghua*** (poo-tohng-hwah) 普通话 or "the common language," as their first or second language. A further boon to foreigners taking up the study of the national Chinese language is the fact that Mandarin Chinese—now the only "dialect" needed—has only four tones. [Some of the other dialects have as many as eight tones.]

Boyé Lafayette De Mente

INTRODUCTON

Chinese Written in "English"

The transcription of Mandarin Chinese into Roman letters, known as ***pinyin*** (peen-een) 拼音, was reformed in 1958, making it easier for foreigners to study the language without having to learn the thousands of ideograms.

However, several of the letters used in the ***pinyin*** version of Chinese are still pronounced in what might the called the old way. These include c, q, x, z, and the combination of ch. C is pronounced more or less as "ts," q as "ch," x as "sh," z as "dz," and zh as "j."

There are also some variations (from English) in the pronunciation of vowels in Chinese words. U may be pronounced more like o, and e may be pronounced more like u. These and other variations in pronunciation are accounted for — to the extent possible — in the English phonetic version of each word and sentence in this book.

Here are some additional guidelines on how the 26 English letters are pronounced when used in Chinese words (most of them are pronounced very much like they are in English):

A   "ah", as in father
B   like the "b" in bay
C   like "ts" in rats
D   similar to the "d" in day
E   similar to the "u" in up
F   same as in English
G   similar to the "g" in gay
H   similar to the "h" in hah
I   pronounced as the "e" in easy

J sounds like "jee-ay"
K like the "k" in kay
L same as in English
M same as in English
N similar to the "n" in nay
O "oh"
P like the "p" in pay
Q sounds like "chee", as in cheese
R same as in English
S same as in English
T has a "ta" sound, as in take
U like the "oo" in oops
W like "wa" in water
X pronounced "she"
Y pronounced like "yah"
Z sounds like the "ds" in heads

Those Notorious "Tones"

Dealing with the problem of tonal changes in the pronunciation of Chinese words remains a challenge, but with a little effort, it does not preclude one from communicating effectively in the language. For one thing, one of the four tones in the language is neutral or flat, requiring no tonal change. [This is the way most English is spoken, but if you enunciate *all* Chinese words in this manner you will get some surprising results!]

Fortunately, the pronunciation of the other three tones in Chinese is not absolutely precise in actual use, although there is an "official" tone. Different people pronounce them slightly differently, so there is some tolerance; plus the fact that the context in which words are used helps make the meaning clear.

The four tones in Mandarin Chinese are described as even, rising, falling-rising, and falling. The even tone is generally spoken in a slightly higher pitch then the normal voice. In the rising tone, the voice goes from the normal pitch to a slightly higher pitch. In the falling-rising tone the voice goes down and up, and in the falling tone the voice goes from a higher to a lower tone.

In "formal" Chinese written in Roman letters the tones are indicated by diacritical marks over the appropriate letters—the even tone by a horizontal line; the rising tone by a line sloping up; the falling-rising tone by a v-shaped mark; and the falling tone by a line slanting downward. When there are no diacritical marks over letters it means they are pronounced "flat."

Again, while using an incorrect tone will change the meaning of a word, pronunciation of the tones by the Chinese themselves often varies significantly, based on their education, where they were raised, etc.

Chinese is Easier Than English!

It may require a stretch to think of Chinese as simpler and easier than English, but linguistically speaking that is the case. The Chinese "alphabet" consists of 405 syllables that use tonal differences to make up some 1,277 "building blocks." English uses 26 letters and 44 basic sounds to create *several thousand* "building blocks."

The 405 Chinese syllables are made up of combinations of five vowel sounds, 23 consonant sounds and 15 compound sounds consisting of combinations of the five vowels. While this may sound extraordinarily intimidating, the same syllables are repeated over and over, and their spelling never changes—while there often appears to be no rhyme or reason to the spelling of English words.

Chinese is also grammatically simpler than English. The sentence order of Chinese is the same as that of English: subject, verb and object. Adjectives come before nouns, just as they do in English. But there are no verb conjugations in Chinese, no articles (the, a, an), and no plurals. To make the Chinese words for I, you, he, she and it plural, you just add the suffix *men* (mern) to them:

I	*wo*	(woh)	我
we	*wo-men*	(woh-mern)	我们
you	*ni*	(nee)	你
you (all)	*ni-men*	(nee-mern)	你们
he, she, it	*ta*	(tah)	他 / 她 / 它
they	*ta-men*	(tah-mern)	他们

There is just one word in Chinese for all of the variations of the verb "to be"—*shi* (pronounced shr) 是, which expresses be, am, is, are and were. Similarly, the word **qu** (chwee) 去, incorporates go, goes, went and gone.

Here are some of the other "rules" of Chinese:

1) The subject of sentences (I, he, she, they, it) is generally not expressed when it is obvious from the context.

2) The past tense is formed by adding the term **le** (ler) 了 after the verb.

3) The future tense is formed by adding the term **jiang** (jee-ahng) 将 before the verb.

4) To make a sentence negative all you do is add the term **bu** (boo) 不 in front of the verb.

5) Questions are formed by the use of interrogative terms and tone of voice as well as by adding the special interrogative term **ma** (mah) 吗 at the end of sentences.

6) Sentences are made possessive by using the word **de** (der) 的 in between the pronoun and noun.

7) Likewise, you qualify adjectives by putting either **bijiao** (bee-jee-ow) 比较 or **zui** (zway) 最 in front of them. **Bijiao** incorporates the meaning of "relatively," and **zui** "most"— in the sense of better and best, bigger and biggest, cheaper, cheapest, etc.

8) Special "measure words" are used between numbers and nouns when referring to a number or quantity of things and people. There are different "measure words" for different types of things (flat, round), for people, animals, etc. There is, however, one "measure word," **ge** (guh) 个 that is more or less universal and may be used for virtually anything if you don't know the correct one.

9) "Yes" and "no" are generally not used by themselves. The custom is to use the negative or the positive of the appropriate verb or adjective to express these meanings. In

other words, the usual response to "Are you going?" is not "no." It is the negative form of going—that is, "not going," with the subject [I] understood—i.e. *qu?* (chwee?) 去 / Are you going? *Bu qu* (boo chwee) 不去 / I'm not going.

There are other "rules" for using Chinese, but rather than trying to remember them individually, it is best to simply use them as they appear in the basic sentences in this book.

The Chinese "Alphabet"

The 405 syllables that make up the Chinese language are in effect the Chinese "alphabet." These syllables are divided into five sets, each of which is based on three or more of the five vowel sounds, *a* (ah), *i* (ee), *u* (uu), *e* (eh) and *o* (oh), combined with consonants.

The initial or first letter in Chinese syllables is always a consonant. The "final" or ending portion of the syllables always begins with a vowel. Example: **sanbu** (sahn-boo), which means walk or stroll. Individual words consist of one or more syllables. And as in English, there are many compound words.

One example of a compound word: **qiche** (chee-cher) 汽车, literally "steam vehicle"; and figuratively, car or automobile. Another commonly seen and used compound word is **xiexie** (she-eh-she-eh) 谢谢, or "thank you." [When pronounced at normal speed it sounds like "shay-shay."]

With only a few exceptions (as shown above) pronounciation of the initial letters of Chinese syllables is the same as or similar to the English pronounciation. Pronounciation of the so-called "final" portions of the syllables varies slightly. [See the pronounciation guidelines below.]

Running Words Together

In written Chinese, characters representing the words of the language are not separated by spaces (as individual words are in English), but because most Chinese words are written with one character, this does not cause the Chinese any problems.

However, the custom of not separating words with spaces is frequently carried over into **pinyin** (the Roman letter version of Chinese), so that what looks like one word may be two or three words, with **Tiananmen**, Beijing's famous central square, being an outstanding example. This is actually three words, written in Chinese with three characters, *Tian An Men* (Tee-an Ahn Mern), which literally means "Heaven Peace Gate," and is usually translated as "Gate of Heavenly Peace."

In some cases in this book, I have chosen to separate the pinyin spellings of some words to make it easier to identify and pronounce them.

Pronouncing Chinese "in English"

The English phonetics used in the following pronunciation guides are designed to approximate the correct Chinese pronunciation as closely as possible. In some cases, the Chinese syllables are pronounced exactly like—or almost exactly like—common English words, and I have chosen to use these English words in an effort to make recognizing and pronouncing syllables and words as simple as possible. The Chinese syllable "**bai**," for example, sounds like "by," and "**bao**" sounds like "bow" (as in bowing down). "**Gai**" sounds like "guy," and so on.

Pronunciation Guide No. 1

[Pronounce the phonetic spellings as English. Note that the *a* (ah) vowel sound is repeated in all of the syllables in this group.]

A *ah*	AI *aye*	AN *in/ahn*	ANG *ahng*	AO *ow* *(as in ouch)*
BA *bah*	BAI *by*	BAN *bahn*	BANG *bahng*	BAO *bow* *(as in bow down)*
CA *tsah*	CAI *tsigh*	CAN *tsahn*	CANG *tsahng*	CAO *tsow*
CHA *chah*	CHAI *chigh*	CHAN *chahn*	CHANG *chahng*	CHAO *chow*
DA *dah*	DAI *die*	DAN *dahn*	DANG *dahng*	DAO *dow*
FA *fah*		FAN *fahn*	FANG *fahng*	
GA *gah*	GAI *guy*	GAN *gahn*	GANG *gahng*	GAO *gow*
HA *hah*	HAI *hi*	HAN *hahn*	HANG *hahng*	HAO *how*
KA *kah*	KAI *kigh*	KAN *kahn*	KANG *kahng*	KAO *kow (as in cow)*
LA *lah*	LAI *lie*	LAN *lahn*	LANG *lahng*	LAO *lao (as in Laos)*

MA	MAI	MAN	MANG	MAO
mah	my	mahn	mahng	mao
NA	NAI	NAN	NANG	NAO
nah	nigh	nahn	nahng	now
PA	PAI	PAN	PANG	PAO
pah	pie	pahn	pahng	pow
		RAN	RANG	RAO
		rahn	rahng	rao
SA	SAI	SAN	SANG	SAO
sah	sigh	sahn	sahng	sao
SHA	SHAI	SHAN	SHANG	SHAO
shah	shy	shahn	shahng	shou
TA	TAI	TAN	TANG	TAO
tah	tie	tahn	tahng	tao
WA	WAI	WAN	WANG	
wah	wigh	wahn	wahng	
YA		YAN	YANG	YAO
yah		yahn	yahng	yee-ow
ZA	ZAI	ZAN	ZANG	ZAO
zah	zigh	zahn	zahng	zow
ZHA	ZHAI	ZHAN	ZHANG	ZHAO
jah	jigh	jahn	jahng	jow

Pronunciation Guide No. 2

[Note that the *e* (eh) vowel sound is repeated in all of the syllables.]

E	EI	EN	ENG	ER
uh	*a**	*ern***	*erng*	*ur*

*EI is pronounced like the "ei" in eight.
**EN is pronounced as the "ern" in concern.

	BEI	BEN	BENG
	bay	*burn*	*bung*
CE		CEN	CENG
tser		*tswun*	*tserng*
CHE		CHEN	CHENG
cher		*churn*	*churng*
DE		DENG	
der		*derng*	
	FEI	FEN	FENG
	fay	*fern*	*ferng*
GE	GEI	GEN	GENG
guh	*gay*	*gurn*	*gurng*
HE	HEI	HEN	HENG
her	*hay*	*hern*	*herng*
KE		KEN	KENG
ker		*kern*	*kerng*

LE *ler*	**LEI** *lay*		**LENG** *lerng*
ME *mer*	**MEI** *may*	**MEN** *mern*	**MENG** *merng*
NE *nuh*	**NEI** *nay*	**NEN** *nern*	**NENG** *nerng*
	PEI *pay*	**PEN** *pern*	**PENG** *perng*
RE *ruh*		**REN** *wren*	**RENG** *wreng*
SE *ser*		**SEN** *sern*	**SENG** *serng*
SHE *sher*	**SHEI** *shay*	**SHEN** *shern*	**SHENG** *sherng*
TE *ter*			**TENG** *terng*
	WEI *way*	**WEN** *wern*	**WENG** *werng*
YE *yeh*			
ZE *zuh*	**ZEI** *zay*	**ZEN** *zern*	**ZENG** *zerng*
ZHE *juh*	**ZHEI** *jay*	**ZHEN** *jern*	**ZHENG** *jehng*

Pronunciation Guide No. 3

[These syllables are based on the *i* vowel sound, which is pronounced as *ee*]

BI	BIAN	BIAO	BIE	BIN	BING
bee	*bee-an**	*bee-ow*	*bee-eh*	*bin*	*beeng*

*Phonetic terms divided by hyphens, like bian (bee-an) should be pronounced smoothly as one word.

CHI					
chee					
CI					
tsu					
DI	DIU	DIAN	DIAO	DIE	DING
dee	*dew/deo*	*dee-an*	*dee-ow*	*dee-eh*	*deeng*
JI	JIA	JIAN	JIAO	JIE	JIN
jee	*jee-ah*	*jee-an*	*jee-ow*	*jee-eh*	*jeen*
JING	JIU	JIANG			
jeeng	*jew/jeo*	*jee-ahng*			
LI		LIAN	LIAO	LIE	LIN
lee		*lee-an*	*lee-ow*	*lee-eh*	*leen*
LING	LIU	LIANG			
leeng	*lew/leo*	*lee-ahng*			
MI		MIAN	MIAO	MIE	MIN
me		*mee-an*	*mee-ow*	*me-eh*	*meen*
MING	MIU				
meeng	*mew*				

NI		NIAN	NIAO	NIE	NIN
nee		*nee-an*	*nee-ow*	*nee-eh*	*neen*
NING	NIU	NIANG			
neeng	*new*	*nee-ahng*			
PI	PIAN	PIAO	PIE	PIN	PING
pee	*pee-an*	*pee-ow*	*pee-eh*	*peen*	*peeng*
QI	QIA	QIAN	QIAO	QIE	QIN
chee	*chee-ah*	*chee-in*	*chee-ow*	*chee-eh*	*cheen*
QING	QIU	QIANG			
cheeng	*chew*	*chee-ahng*			
RI					
rr					
SHI					
shr					
SI					
suh					
TI		TIAN	TIAO	TIE	TING
tee		*tee-an*	*tee-ow*	*tee-eh*	*teeng*
XI	XIA	XIAN	XIAO	XIE	XIN
she	*she-ah*	*shee-an*	*she-ow*	*she-eh*	*sheen*
XING	XIU	XIANG	XIONG		
sheeng	*shew*	*shee-ahng*	*she-ong*		
YI				YIN	YING
ee				*een*	*eeng*
ZHI	ZI				
jr	*dzu*				

Pronunciation Guide No. 4

[These syllables are based on the *o* (oh) vowel sound]

BO *bwo/bwough*			
CHONG *chohng*	CHOU *choe*	CONG *tsohng*	COU *tsoe*
		DONG *doong*	DOU *doe*
FO *fwo/fwough*	FOU *foe*		
		GONG *gohng*	GOU *go*
		HONG *hohng*	HOU *hoe*
		KONG *kohng*	KOU *koe*
		LONG *lohng*	LOU *low*
		MO *mwo/mwough*	MOU *moe*
		NONG *nohng*	

O *aw*			**OU** *oh*
PO *pwaw*			
		RONG *rohng*	**ROU** *roe*
	SHOU *show*	**SONG** *sohng*	
		TONG *tohng*	**TOU** *toe*
WO *woh*			
YO *yaw*		**YONG** *yohng*	**YOU** *you*
ZHONG *johng*	**ZHOU** *joe*	**ZONG** *zohng*	**ZOU** *dzow*

Pronunciation Guide No. 5

[These syllables are based on the *u* ("oo" as in soon) vowel sound.]

BU *boo*			
CHU *choo*		**CHUAI** *chwie*	**CHUAN** *chwahn*
CHUANG *chwang*	**CHUI** *chwee/chway*	**CHUN** *choon*	**CHUO** *chwoh*
CU *tsu*		**CUAN** *tswahn*	
	CUI *tsway/tswee*	**CUN** *tsoon*	**CUO** *tswoh*
DU *doo*		**DUAN** *dwahn*	**DUI** *dway/dwee*
	DUN *doon*	**DUO** *dwoh*	
FU *foo*			
GU *goo*	**GUA** *gwah*	**GUAI** *gwie*	**GUAN** *gwahn*
GUANG *gwahng*	**GUI** *gway/gwee*	**GUN** *goon*	**GUO** *gwoh*
HU *hoo*	**HUA** *hway*	**HUAI** *hwie*	**HUAN** *hwahn*
HUANG *hwahng*	**HUI** *hway/hwee*	**HUN** *hoon*	**HUO** *hwoh*

JU *jwee*			**JUAN** *jwen*
	JUE *jway*	**JUN** *jwin/joon*	
KU *koo*	**KUA** *kwah*	**KUAI** *kwie*	**KUAN** *kwahn*
KUANG *kwahng*	**KUI** *kway/kwee*	**KUN** *koon*	**KUO** *kway*
LU *loo or lwee*			**LUAN** *lwahn*
	LUE *lu-eh*	**LUN** *loon*	**LUO** *lwaw*
MU *moo*			
NU *nwee*			**NUAN** *nwahn*
	NUE *nu-eh*		**NUO** *nwoh*
PU *poo*			
QU *chwee*	**QUE** *chee-eh*		**QUAN** *chwahn*
		QUN *chwun*	
RU *roo*			**RUAN** *rwahn*
	RUI *rway/rwee*	**RUN** *roon*	**RUO** *rwoh*

SHU *shoo*	**SHUA** *shwah*	**SHUAI** *shwie*	**SHUAN** *shwahn*
SHUANG *shwahng*	**SHUI** *shway/shwee*	**SHUN** *shoon*	**SHUO** *shwo*
SU *soo*			**SUAN** *swahn*
	SUI *sway/swee*	**SUN** *soon*	**SUO** *swoh*
TU *too*			**TUAN** *twahn*
	TUI *tway*	**TUN** *toon*	**TUO** *twoh*
WU *woo*			
XU *shee*			**XUAN** *shwen*
	XUE *shu-eh*	**XUN** *sheen*	
YU *yuu*			**YUAN** *ywahn*
	YUE *yu-eh*	**YUN** *ywun*	
ZHU *joo*	**ZHUA** *jwah*	**ZHUAI** *jwie*	**ZHUAN** *jwahn*
ZHUANG *jwahng*	**ZHUI** *jway/jwee*	**ZHUN** *joon*	**ZHUO** *jwoh*
ZU *joo*			**ZUAN** *zwahn*
	ZUI *zway/zwee*	**ZUN** *zwun*	**ZUO** *zwoh*

PART 1

Common Expressions & Key Words

Please keep in mind that the phonetic words that are divided by hyphens [to make the syllables easier to recognize] should be pronounced as single words, in a smooth, even flow.

Hello (also used in the sense of How are you?)
Nin hao! 您好！
(Neen how)

[*Nin hao (neen how)* and the informal *ni hao (nee how)* are commonly used as universal greetings (good morning, good afternoon, good evening), but there are also specific words for these expressions.]

Good morning!
Zaoshang hao! 早上好！
(Zow-shahng how)

Good afternoon!
Xiawu hao! 下午好！
(Shee-ah-woo how)

Good evening!
Wanshang hao! 晚上好！
(Wahn-shahng how)

Good night!
Wan an! 晚安！
(Wahn ahn)

See you tomorrow.
Mingtian jian. 明天见。
(Meeng-tee-an jee-an)

See you later.
Yi huir jian. 一会儿见。
(Ee hway-er jee-an)

Goodbye.
Zai jian. 再见。
(Zigh jee-an)

OK.
Xing. 行。
(Sheeng)

Please.
Qing. 请。
(Cheeng)

Thank you.
Xie Xie. 谢谢。
(She-eh She-eh, sounds like *shay-shay)*

Thank you for your hospitality.
Duoxie ni dekuandai. 多谢你的款待。
(Dwoh-she-eh nee der-kwahn-die)

Thank you for your kindness.
Duoxie ni de haoyi. 多谢你的好意。
(Dwoh-she-eh nee der how-ee)

You're welcome.
Bu xie.　不谢。
(Boo she-eh)

Don't mention it.
Bu keqi meiyou guanxi.　不客气，没有关系。
(Boo ker-chee may-you gwahn-she)

I'm sorry.
Duibuqi.　对不起。
(Dway-boo-chee)

That's all right.
Mei guanxi.　没关系。
(May gwahn-she)

That's right.
Duile.　对了。
(Dway-ler)

That's wrong.
Bu dui.　不对。
(Boo dway)

Very good.
Hen hao.　很好。
(Hern how)

Excellent!
Hao ji le!　好及了！
(How jee ler)

Yes, I agree; correct 是；对
Shi (shr); Dui (dway)

Yes **You** *(You)* 有

No *Bu shi (Boo shr)* 不是

I understand.
Wo dong.   我懂。
(Woh dohng)

Do you understand?
Dong ma?   懂吗？
(Dohng mah)

I don't understand.
Wo bu dong.   我不懂。
(Woh boo dohng)

Do you speak English?
Ni hui Yingyu ma?   你会英语吗？
(Nee hway Eeng-yuu mah)

Also: *Ni dong bu dong Yingyu?*   你懂不懂英语？
(Nee dohng boo dohng Eeng-yuu)

Please repeat that.
Qing ni zaishuo yibian.   请你再说一遍。
(Cheeng nee zigh-shwoh ee-bee-an)

Please speak more slowly.
Qing ni shuo man dian.   请你说慢点。
(Cheeng nee shwo mahn dee-an)

I, me   *wo (woh)* 我

I am going.
Wo yao qu.   我要去。
(Woh yee-ow chwee)

I'm not going.
Bu qu.   不去
(Boo chwee)

I'm lost!
Wo mi lu le!   我迷路了！
(Woh me loo ler)

I'm looking for my friends.
Wo zai zhao wo-de pengyou.   我在找我的朋友。
(Woh zigh jow woh-der perng-you)

we   *wo-men (woh-mern)*   我们

We're lost!
Wo-men mi lu le!   我们迷路了！
(Woh-mern me loo ler)

my, mine   *wo-de (woh-der)*   我的

This is mine.
Zhe shi wo-de.   这是我的。
(Juh shr woh-der)

That is not mine.
Bu shi wo-de.   不是我的。
(Boo shr woh-der)

you *ni (nee)*, informal 你
nin (neen), polite 您

How are you?
Nin hao ma? 您好吗？
(Neen how mah)

Fine, thank you.
Hen hao, xiexie. 很好，谢谢。
(Hern how, she-eh she-eh)

And you?
Ni ne? 你呢？
(Nee nuh)

Who are you?
Ni shi shei? 你是谁？
(Nee shr shay)

you (plural) *nimen (nee-mern)* 你们
your *ni-de (nee-der)* 你的

That is your umbrella.
Na shi ni-de san. 那是你的伞。
(Nah shr nee-der sahn)

your (plural) *nimen-de (nee-mern-der)* 你们的
he, she, it *ta (tah)* 他／她／它

He/she is not going.
Ta bu qu. 他／她不去。
(Tah boo chwee)

| his, hers, its | *ta-de* (tah-der) 他的 / 她的 / 它的 |
| we, us | *wo-men* (woh-mern) 我们 |

We are not going.
Wo-men bu qu.   我们不去。
(Woh-mern boo chwee)

our	*wo-men-de* (woh-mern-der) 我们的
they, them	*ta-men* (tah-mern) 他们
their, theirs	*ta-men-de* (tah-mern-der) 他们的
what	*shenme* (shern-mer) 什么
this	*zhe* (juh); 这 *zhei* (jay) 这

What is this?
Zhe shi shenme?   这是什么？
(Juh shr shern-mer)

This is his/her book.
Zhe shi ta-de shu.   这是他 / 她的书。
(Juh shr tah-der shoo)

What is your email address?
Ni-de dianzi youjian xinxiang shi shenme?
(Nee-der dee-an-dzu you-jee-an sheen-she-ahng she-shern-mer)
你的电子邮件信箱是什么？

| that | *na* (nah) 那 |

What is that?
Na shi shenme?   那是什么？
(Nah shr shern-mer)

I don't want that.
Wo bu yao na ge. 我不要那个。
(Woh boo yee-ow nah guh)

who?   *shui?* *(shway)* 谁?
                 shei? *(shay)* 谁?

Who is it?
Shei? 谁?
(Shay)

when?
shenme shihou? 什么时候?
(shern-mer shr-hoe)

When are we going?
Wo-men shenme shihou qu? 我们什么时候去?
(Woh-mern shern-mer shr-hoe chwee)

where?   *nali?* *(nah-lee)* 那里?;
                 nar? *(nah-urr)* 那儿?

Where are we going?
Wo-men yao qu nali? 我们要去那里?
(Woh-mern yee-ow chwee nah-lee)

Where is the toilet?
Nali you cesuo? 那里有厕所?
(Nah-lee you tser-swoh)

Where is the men's room?
Nali you nan cesuo? 那里有男厕所?
(Nah-lee you nahn tser-swoh)

Where is the ladies' room?
Nali you nu cesuo?　那里有女厕所？
(Nah-lee you nwee tser-swoh)

Where is a public telephone?
Gongyong dianhua zai nali?　公用电话在那里？
(Gohng-yohng dee-an-hwah zigh nah-lee)

why?　　　　　　　*weishenme? (way-shern-mer)* 为什么？

Why have we stopped?
Wo-men weishenme tingxia?　我们为什么停下？
(Woh-mern way-shern-mer teeng-shee-ah)

how　　　　　　　*duo (dwoh)* 多；*duome (dwoh-mer)* 多么；
　　　　　　　　　　zenme (zern-mer) 怎么；*jige (jee-guh)* 几个

How far is it?
Li zhe duo yuan?　离这多远？
(Lee juh dwoh ywahn)

How long will it take?
Zhe yao duo jiu?　这要多久？
(Juh yee-ow dwoh jeo)

which?　　　　　　*neige? (nay-guh)* 那个？；
　　　　　　　　　　nage? (nah-guh) 那个？

Which one?
Na yi-ge?　那一个？
(Nah yee-guh)

have   *you (you)* 有

Do you have _____?
Youmei you _____? 有没有 _____ ?
(You-may-you _____)

good / well   *hao (how)* 好

I don't feel well.
Wo gan jue bu hao. 我感觉不好。
(Woh gahn jway boo how)

I need an interpreter!
Wo xuyao fanyi! 我需要翻译！
(Woh shee-yee-ow fahn-ee)

wait   *deng (derng)* 等

Please wait a minute.
Qing deng yi xia. 请等一下。
(Cheeng derng ee shee-ah)

Just a second!
Deng yi deng! 等一等！
(Derng ee derng)

I'm sorry, I cannot wait.
Duibuqi, wo bu neng deng. 对不起，我不能等。
(Dway-boo-chee, woh boo nerng derng)

Hurry up!
Gan kuai! 赶快！
(Gahn kwie)

I don't know.
Wo bu zhidao.　我不知道。
(Woh boo jr-dow)

Is that so?
Shi-ma?　是吗？
(Shr-mah)

I think so.
Wo xiang shi-de.　我想是的。
(Woh she-ahng shr-der)

I don't think so.
Wo bu renwei shi zheyang.　我不认为是这样。
(Woh boo wren-way shr juh-yahng)

It doesn't matter.
Mei guan xi.　没关系。
(May gwahn she)

No problem.
Mei wenti.　没问题。
(May wern-tee)

This is mine.
Zhe shi wo-de.　这是我的。
(Juh shr woh-der)

That is my luggage.
Na shi wo-de xingli.　那是我的行李。
(Nah shr woh-der sheeng-lee)

What is that?
Na shi shenme? 那是什么？
(Nah shr shern-mer)

What time is it?
Ji dian-le? 几点了？
(Jee dee-an-ler)

What time shall I come?
Wo gai shenme shihou lai? 我该什么时候来？
(Woh guy shern-mer shr-how lie)

When are you going?
Ni shenme shihou qu? 你什么时候去？
(Nee shern-mer shr-hoe chwee)

Where is it?
Ta zai nali? 它在那里？
(Tah zigh nah-lee)

How much (is it)?
Duo shao? 多少？
(Dwoh show)

How far is it?
Li zhe duo yuan? 离这多远？
(Lee juh dwoh ywahn)

Which one?
Na yi-ge? 那一个？
(Nah yee-guh)

buy   *mai (my)* 买

I want to buy this.
Wo xiang mai zhe ge.   我想买这个。
(Woh shee-ahng my juh guh)

drink (verb)   *he (her)* 喝

I would like to drink something cold.
Wo xing he dian liang-de yinliao.   我想喝点凉的饮料。
(Woh shee-ahng her dee-an lee-ahng der een-lee-ow)

I do not drink alcoholic drinks.
Wo bu he jiu.   我不喝酒。
(Woh boo her jeo)

eat   *chi (chr)* 吃

What time do we eat?
Wo-men shenme shi jian chi fan?   我们什么时间吃饭？
(Woh-mern shern-mer shr jee-an chr fahn)

Where shall we go to eat?
Women qu nali chi?   我们去那里吃？
(Woh-mern chwee nah-lee chr)

like   *xihuan (she-hwahn)* 喜欢

I like Chinese food.
Xihuan zhong can.   我喜欢中餐。
(She-hwahn johng tsahn)

I don't like it.
Bu xihuan.   不喜欢。
(Boo she-hwahn)

I can't eat this!
Wo bu neng chi zhe-ge!   我不能吃这个！
(Woh boo nerng chr juh-guh)

enough   *gou-le (go-ler)*   够了

That's enough!
Na xie gou-le!   那些够了！
(Nah she-eh go-luh)

I have had enough.
Wo chi gou-le.   我吃够了。
(Woh chr go-ler)

a little   *yidian dianr (ee-dee-an dee-an-urr)*
一点点儿

Just a little, please.
Jiu yidian dianr.   就一点点儿。
(Jeo ee-dee-an dee-an-urr)

too much   *tai dou-le (tie dwoh-ler)* 太多了

That's too much!
Na xie tai duo-le!   那些太多了！
(Nah she-eh tie dwoh-ler)

go　　　　　*qu (chwee)* 去

Are you going?
Ni qu ma?　你去吗？
(Nee chwee mah)

I'm not going.
Bu qu.　不去。
(boo chwee)

I want to go to a shopping district.
Wo xiang qu mai dongxi.　我想去买东西。
(Woh shee-ang chwee my dohng she)

Can you go with me?
Ni neng he wo yiqi qu ma?　你能和我一起去吗？
(Nee nerng her woh ee-chee chwee mah)

I cannot go now.
Wo xianzai bu neng qu.　我现在不能去。
(Woh shee-an-zigh boo nerng chwee)

have　　　　　*you (you)* 有

Do you have it?
Ni you ma?　你有吗？
(Nee you mah)

I don't have it!
Wo mei you!　我没有！
(Woh may you)

look/see   *kan (kahn)* 看

May I see it?
Wo neng kan ma? 我能看吗？
(Woh nerng kahn mah)

mistake   *cuowu (tswoh-woo)* 错误

I made a mistake.
Wo zuo-le yijian cuoshi. 我做了一件错事。
(Woh zwoh-ler ee-jee-an tswoh-shr)

I think that is a mistake.
Wo xiang na shi-ge cuowu. 我想那是个错误。
(Woh shee-ahng nah shr-guh tswoh-woo)

Can you help me?
Neng bang wo yixia ma? 能帮我一下吗？
(Nerng bahng woh ee-shee-ah mah)

Excuse me! (to get attention)
Lao jia! 劳驾！
(Lao jee-ah)

May I ask you a question?
Neng wen ni yi ge wenti ma? 能问你一个问题吗？
(Nerng wern nee ee guh wern-tee mah)

write   *xie (she-eh)* 写

Please write it down for me.
Qing xie xia lai. 请写下来。
(Cheeng she-eh she-ah lie)

Please write it in Roman letters.
Qing yong pinyin xie. 请用拼音写。
(Cheeng yohng peen-een she-eh)

Please write it in Chinese.
Qing yong Zhongwen xie. 请用中文写。
(Cheeng yohng Johng-wern she-eh)

want   *yao (yee-ow)* 要

What do you want?
Ni yao shenme? 你要什么？
(Nee yee-ow shern-mer)

Congratulations!
Zhuhe ni! 祝贺你！
(Joo-her nee)

Look out!
Xiao xin! 小心！
(She-ow sheen)

Help!
Jiu ming a! 救命啊！
(Jeo meeng ah)

Please call an ambulance!
Qing kuai jiao jiuhu che! 请快叫救护车！
(Cheeng kwai jee-ow jeo-hoo cher)

Please take me back to my hotel.
Qing kuai song wo hui luguan. 请快送我回旅馆。
(Cheeng kwai sohng woh hway lwee-gwahn)

big, large	*da (dah)* 大	
large size	*da hao (dah how)* 大号	
medium size	*zhong hao (johng how)* 中号	
small size	*xiao hao (shee-ow how)* 小号	

It's too big.
Zhe tai da-le. 这太大了。
(Juh tie dah-ler)

cheap	*pianyi (pee-an-ee)* 便宜	
expensive	*gui (gway)* 贵	

That one is too expensive.
Na yi-ge tai gui. 那一个太贵。
(Nah ee-guh tie gway)

long   *chang (chahng)* 长

The sleeves are too long.
Xiuzi tai chang-le. 袖子太长了。
(Shew dzu tie chahng-ler)

short   *duan (dwahn)* 短

The sleeves are too short.
Xiuzi tai duan-le. 袖子太短了。
(Shew dzu tie dwahn-ler)

small	*xiao (she-ow)* 小	
best	*zuihao (zway-how)* 最好	

This the best (one).
Zhe zuihao.　这最好。
(Juh zwee-how)

better
geng hao　更好
(gurng how)

Personal Information

family name   *xing (sheeng)* 姓

My name is George.
Wo jiao George.   我叫 George。
(Woh jee-ow George)

What is your name?
Ni jiao shenme mingzi?   你叫什么名字？
(Nee jee-ow shern-mer meeng-dzu)

family name   *mingzi (meeng-dzu)* 名字
full name   *xingming (sheeng-meeng)* 姓名
address   *dizhi (dee-jr)* 地址

What is your address?
Ni de dizhi shi shenme?   你的地址是什么？
(Nee der jee-jr shr shern-mer)

age   *nianling (nee-an-leeng)* 年龄
name   *ming zi (meeng dzu)* 名字
husband   *zhangfu / airen (jahng-foo / aye-wren)* 丈夫 /
           爱人
wife   *qizi / furen / airen (chee-dzu / foo-wren / aye-*
           wren) 妻子 / 夫人 / 爱人
my husband *wo-de airen (woh-der aye-wren)* 我的爱人

This is my husband.
Zhe shi wo-de airen.   这是我的爱人。
(Juh shr woh-der aye-wren)

My wife   *wo-de furen (woh-der foo-wren)* 我的夫人

This is my wife.
Zhe shi wo-de furen.   这是我的夫人。
(Juh shr woh-der foo-wren)

Our son.
Wo-men-de erzi.   我们的儿子。
(Woh-mern-der urr-jee)

Our daughter.
Wo-men-de nuer.   我们的女儿。
(Woh-mern-derh nwee-urr)

We are from Arizona.
Wo-men shi Arizona lai-de.   我们是 Arizona 来的。
(Woh-mern shr Arizona lie-der)

Are you married?
Ni jiehun le ma?   你结婚了吗？
(Nee jee-eh-hoon ler mah)

Do you have children?
Ni you xiaohai ma?   你有小孩吗？
(Nee you she-ow-high mah)

Please give me your phone number.
Qing gaosu wo ni-de dianhua haoma.
请告诉我你的电话号码。
(Cheeng gow-soo woh nee-der dee-an-hwah how-mah)

What is your email address?
Ni-de dianzi youjian xinxiang shishenme?
(Nee-der dee-an-dzu you-jee-an sheen-she-ahng shr-shern-mer)
你的电子邮件信箱是什么？

May I take your picture?
Wo gei ni zhaoxiang hao ma? 我给你照相好吗？
(Woh gay nee jow-she-ahng how mah)

Directions

north	*bei (bay)* 北
east	*dong (dohng)* 东
south	*nan (nahn)* 南
west	*xi (she)* 西
northeast	*dongbei (dohng-bay)* 东北
southeast	*dongnan (dohng-nahn)* 东南
northwest	*xibei (she-bay)* 西北
southwest	*xinan (she-nahn)* 西南
right	*you (you)* 右
left	*zuo (zwoh)* 左
turn	*guaiwan (gwie-wahn)* 拐弯

Airport / Airline

airport   *feijichang (fay-jee-chahng)* 飞机场

I want to go to the airport.
Wo yao qu feijichang. 我要去飞机场。
(Woh yow chwee fay-jee-chahng)

airport shuttle bus	*jichang jie songche (jee-chahng jee-eh sohng-cher)* 机场接送车
airplane	*feiji (fay-jee)* 飞机
airline	*hangkong gongsi (hahng-kohng gohng-suh)* 航空公司
first class	*toudeng cang (toe-derng tsahng)* 头等舱
business class	*gongwu cang (gohng-woo tsahng)* 公务舱
economy class	*jingji cang (jeeng-jee tsahng)* 经济舱
one-way	*dancheng (dahn-cherng)* 单程
round-trip	*laihui (lie-hway)* 来回
flight	*hangban (hahng-bahn)* 航班
flight number	*hangban haoma (hahng-bahn how-mah)* 航班号码
connecting flight	*xianjie hangban (shee-an jee-eh hahng-bahn)* 线接航班
reservations	*yuding (yuu-deeng)* 预定
confirm	*queren (chwee-eh-wren)* 确认
check-in	*ban chengji shouxu (bahn churng-jee show-shee)* 办乘机手续

I have only carry-on baggage.
Wo zhi you shou tibao. 我只有手提包。
(Woh jr you show tee-bow)

check-in time
jianpiao shijian 剪票时间
(jee-an pee-ow shr-jee-an)

I would like an aisle seat.
Wo xiang yao kao zoudao de weizi. 我想要靠走道的位子。
(Woh she-ahng yee-ow kow dzow dow der way-dzu)

I would like a window seat.
Wo xiang yao kao chuang de weizi. 我想要靠窗的位子。
(Woh she-ahng yee-ow kow chwahng der way-dzu)

boarding time	*qifei shijian (chee-fay shr-jee-an)* 起飞时间
departure time	*chugang shijian (choo-gahng shr-jee-an)* 出岗时间
baggage	*xingli (sheeng-lee)* 行李
claim check	*xingli piao (sheeng-lee-pee-ow)* 行李票
hotel shuttle bus	*luguan jie songche (lwee-gwahn jee-eh sohng-cher)* 旅馆接送车

Money

China's currency is known as **renminbi** (*wren-meen-bee*), which literally means "people's money." The formal Chinese equivalent of the English word "dollar" is **yuan** (*ywahn*). The informal term for this denomination is **kuai** (*kwie*).

The yuan is made up of 100 **fen** (*fern*), and 10 **mao** (*mao*), with the latter commonly referred to as **jiao** (*jee-ow*). The currency comes in 1, 2 and 5 **fen** coins, and 1, 5, 10 and 50 **yuan** notes or bills. There are two Chinese words for cash:

cash	**xiankuan** (*shee-an-kwahn*) 现款	
cash	**xianjin** (*shee-an-jeen*) 现金	
1 yuan	**yi yuan** (*ee-ywahn*) 一元	
	yi kuai (*ee kwie*) 一块	
2 yuan	**liang yuan** (*lee-ahng ywahn*) 两元	
	liang kuai (*lee-ahng kwie*) 两块	
3 yuan	**san yuan** (*sahn ywahn*) 三元	
	san kuai (*sahn kwie*) 三块	
4 yuan	**si yuan** (*suh ywahn*) 四元	
	si kuai (*suh kwie*) 四块	
5 yuan	**wu yuan** (*woo ywahn*) 五元	
	wu kuai (*woo kwie*) 五块	
10 yuan	**shi yuan** (*shr ywahn*) 十元	
	shi kuai (*shr kwie*) 十块	
credit card	**xingyong ka** (*sheen-yohng kah*) 信用卡	

Which credit cards do you accept?
Nimen jieshou naxie xingyongka? 你们接受那些信用卡？
(Nee-mern jee-eh-show nah-shee-ah sheeng-yohng kah)

| traveler's checks | *luxing zhipiao* (lwee-sheeng jr-pee-ow) 旅行支票 |
| signature | *qianming* (chee-an meeng) 签名 |

Where do I sign?
Zai nali qian zi? 在那里签字？
(Zigh nah-lee chee-an dzu)

US dollars	*Mei yuan* (May ywahn) 美元
British Sterling	*Ying bang* (Eeng bahng) 英镑
Deutsche Mark	*Xide Make* (She-der Mah-ker) 西德马克
Hong Kong dollars	*Gang bi* (Gahng bee) 港币
Japanese yen	*Ri yuan* (Ree ywahn) 日元
Australian dollars	*Aodaliya yuan* (Ow-dah-lee-yah ywahn) 奥地利亚元
exchange	*duihuan* (dway-hwahn) 兑换
exchange rate	*duihuan lu* (dway-hwahn lwee) 兑换率
exchange money	*duihuan qian* (dway-hwahn chee-an) 兑换钱
small change	*ling qian* (leeng chee-an) 零钱
small bills	*xiao chaopiao* (she-ow chow-pee-ow) 小钞票
large bills	*da chaopiao* (dah chow-pee-ow) 大钞票
money	*qian* (chee-an) 钱

Where can I exchange money?
Nali keyi duihuan qian? 那里可以兑换钱？
(Nah-lee ker-ee dway-hwahn chee-an)

What is today's exchange rate for U.S. dollars?
Jintian Mei yuan duihuan lu duosho? 今天美元兑换率多少？
(Jeen-tee-an May ywahn dway-hwahn lwee dwoh-shou)

Can you cash a personal check?
Keyi duihuan siren zhipiao ma? 可以兑换私人支票吗？
(Ker-ee dway-hwahn suh-wren jr-pee-ow mah)

automatic teller machine (atm)   *tikuan ji (tee-kwahn jee)*
提款机

tip   *xiaofei (she-ow-fay)* 小费

Where is an ATM?
Nali you tikuan ji? 那里有提款机？
(Nah-lee you tee-kwahn jee)

Will it accept foreign bank cards?
Shou waiguo yinhang ka ma? 收外国银行卡吗？
(Show wigh-gwoh een-hang kah mah)

How much should I tip?
Yinggai gei duoshao xiaofei? 应该给多少小费？
(Eeng-guy gay dwoh-shou she-ow-fay)

Is foreign currency okay?
Keyi yong waibi gei ma? 可以用外币给吗？
(Ker-ee yohng wigh-bee gay mah)

This (tip) is for you.
Zhe shi gei ni-de. 这是给你的。
(Juh she gay nee-der)

Taxis

taxi   *chuzuche (choo-joo-cher)* 出租车
taxi stand   *chuzuche zhan (choo-joo-cher jahn)* 出租车站
fare   *chefei (cher-fay)* 车费

Please call a taxi for me.
Qing gei wo jiao che. 请给我叫车。
(Cheeng gay woh jee-ow cher)

I want to go to _____
Wo yao qu _____ 我要去 _____
(Woh yow chwee _____)

Please go to _____
Qing qu _____ 请去 _____
(Cheeng chwee _____)

Is it far?
Hen yuan ma? 很远吗？
(Hern ywahn mah)

Please wait for me.
Qing deng wo yixia. 请等我一下。
(Cheeng derng woh ee-she-ah)

I will be right back.
Wo mashang jiu huilai. 我马上就回来。
(Woh mah-shahng jeo hway-lie)

How much is it to Tiananmen Square?
Qu Tiananmen duoshao qian? 去天安门多少钱？
(Chwee tee-an-ahn-mern dwoh-shou chee-an)

The airport, please.
Qing qu jichang. 请去机场。
(Cheeng chwee jee-chahng)

Please turn on the meter.
Qing da biao. 请打表。
(Cheeng dah bee-ow)

How much do I owe you?
Wo gai fu ni duoshao? 我该付你多少？
(Woh guy foo nee dwoh-shou)

Please give me a receipt.
Qing gei wo kai shouju. 请给我开收据。
(Cheeng gay woh kigh show-jwee)

Subways

subway   *ditie (dee-tee-eh)* 地铁
subway station   *ditie chezhan (dee-tee-eh cher-jahn)*
地铁车站

Where is the nearest subway station?
Zuijin de ditie chezhan zai nali? 最近的地铁车站在那里？
(Zway-jeen der dee-tee-eh cher-jahn zigh nah-lee)

Where is the subway entrance?
Ditie zhankou zai nali 地铁站口在那里？
(Dee-tee-eh jahn-koe zigh nah-lee)

Trains

Trains are the primary means of long-distance travel in China, and although often crowded they offer an extraordinary opportunity to meet people and see the picturesque countryside.

Chinese National Railways	*Zhongguo Tielu (Johng-gwoh Tee-eh-loo)* 中国铁路
train	*huoche (hwoh-cher)* 火车
train station	*huoche zhan (hwoh-cher jahn)* 火车站
local train	*putong che (poo-tohng cher)* 普通车
express train	*kuai che (kwie cher)* 快车
special express	*te kuai (ter kwie)* 特快
ticket	*piao (pee-ow)* 票
adult ticket	*daren piao (dah-wren pee-ow)* 大人票
ticket office	*shou piao chu (show pee-ow choo)* 售票处
one-way ticket	*dan cheng piao (dahn churng pee-ow)* 单程票
round-trip ticket	*laihui piao (lie-hway pee-ow)* 来回票
first-class ticket	*tou-deng piao (toe-derng pee-ow)* 头等票
economy-class ticket	*putong piao (poo-tohng pee-ow)* 普通票

*First-class accommodations on trains and ships are generally called "soft" class. Second and third class accommodations are called "hard" class.

compartment	*chexiang (cher-shee-ahng)* 车厢
reserved seat ticket	*yuding zuowei piao (yuu-deeng zwoh-way pee-ow)* 预定座位票
unreserved seat ticket	*wu yuding zuowei piao (woo yuu-deeng zwoh pee-ow)* 无预定座位票
waiting room	*houche shi (hoe-cher shr)* 候车室
boarding platform	*yuetai (yu-eh-tie)* 月台
get on board	*shang che (shahng cher)* 上车
get off train	*xia (she-ah)* 下
disembark	*xiache (she-ah cher)* 下车
departure time	*likai shi jian (lee-kigh shr-jee-an)* 离开时间
arrival time	*daoda shijian (dow-dah shr-jee-an)* 到达时间
dining car	*can che (tsahn cher)* 餐车
transfer	*dao (dow)* 倒; *huan (hwahn)* 换
stop	*ting (teeng)* 停

Where is the train station?
Che zhan zai nali? 车站在那里?
(Cher jahn zigh nah-lee)

Where is the ticket office?
Nali shi shou piao chu? 那里是售票处?
(Nah-lee shr show pee-ow choo)

Which platform?
Neige yuetai? 那个月台?
(Nay-guh yuu-eh-tie)

Where is the dining car?
Can che zai nali? 餐车在那里?
(Tsahn cher zigh nah-lee)

Does the train have Western-style toilets?
You Xishi-de cesuo ma? 有西式的厕所吗？
(You She-shr-der tser-swoh mah)

Where is the toilet?
Cesuo zai nali? 厕所在那里？
(Tser-swoh zigh nah-lee)

Is this seat taken?
Zhe weizi you ren zuo ma? 这位子有人坐吗？
(Juh way-dzu you wren zwoh mah)

Buses

bus	*qiche (chee-cher)* 汽车
bus driver	*siji (suh-jee)* 司机
bus station	*qiche zhongzhang (chee-cher zohng-jahng)* 汽车终站
bus stop	*qiche zhan (chee-cher jahn)* 汽车站
express bus	*kuaiche (kwie-cher)* 快车
fare	*chefei (cher-fay)* 车费

Where is the bus stop?
Qiche zhongzhan zai nali? 汽车终站在那里？
(Chee-cher johng-jahng zigh nah-lee)

Is it far from here?
Li zheli yuan ma? 离这里远吗？
(Lee juh-lee ywahn mah)

How many stops (from here)?
Ji zhan? 几站？
(Jee jahn)

Is it necessary to change buses?
Yao huan che ma? 要换车吗？
(Yee-ow hwahn cher mah)

Please tell me where to get off.
Qing gaosu wo zai nali xia che. 请告诉我在那里下车。
(Cheeng gow-soo woh zigh nah-lee she-ah cher)

Rental Cars

rent   *zu joo* 租
car   *che cher* 车

I want to rent a car.
Wo yao zu yi liang che. 我要租一辆车。
(Woh yee-ow joo ee lee-ahng cher)

Do you charge by time or mileage?
An shijian suan, haishi an licheng? 按时间算, 还是按里程？
(An shr-jee-an swahn, high-shr ahn lee-churng)

What is the charge by the day?
Meitian zujin duoshao? 每天租金多少？
(May-tee-an joo-jeen dwoh-shou)

Does the price include gasoline?
Jiaqian baokuo qiyou fei ma? 价钱包括汽油费吗？
(Jee-ah-chee-an bow-kwoh chee-you fay mah)

Does the price include insurance?
Feiyong baokuo baoxian ma? 费用包括保险吗？
(Fay-yohng bow-kwoh bow-shee-an mah)

I want to buy insurance.
Wo xiang mai baoxian. 我想买保险。
(Woh she-ahng my bow-shee-an)

Hotel Vocabulary

There are several words for hotels in Chinese, depending on the type and age. Older hotels may be called "place for guests" or "place for eating."

Hotel (place for travelers)   *luguan** *(lwee-gwahn)* 旅馆
                                     ludian *(lwee-dee-an)* 旅店
Hotel (place for guests)   *binguan* *(bin-gwahn)* 宾馆
Hotel (place for eating)   *fandian* *(fahn-dee-an)* 饭店
Hotel (place for liquor)   *jiudian* *(jeo-dee-an)* 酒店

* *Luguan (lwee-gwahn)* is now the common generic term for hotel.

vacancy (rooms available)   *fangjian (fahng-jee-an)* 房间
reservations   *yuding (yuu-deeng)* 预定
check in (register)   *dengji (derng-jee)* 登记
registration desk   *dengji tai (derng-jee tie)* 登记台
lobby   *qianting (chee-an-teeng)* 前厅
check out   *tuifang (tway-fahng)* 退房
cashier   *chunayuan (choo-nah-ywahn)* 出纳员
bell desk   *fuwu tai (foo-woo tie)* 服务台
room key   *yaoshi (yee-ow shr)* 钥匙
room number   *fangjian haoma (fahng-jee-an how-mah)* 房间号码
single room   *dan jian (dahn jee-an)* 单间
double room   *shuangren fang (shwahng-wren fahng)* 双人房
airconditioning   *kongtiao (kohng-tee-ow)* 空调
                                       lengqi (lerng-chee) 冷气
dining room   *can ting (tsahn teeng)* 餐厅

coffee shop	*kafei dian* (kah-fay dee-an)	咖啡店
bar	*jiuba* (jeo-bah)	酒吧

I have a reservation.
Wo yuding le fangjian. 我预定了房间。
(Woh yuu-deeng ler fahng-jee-an)

My (family) name is De Mente.
Wo-de mingzi shi De Mente. 我的名字是 De Mente。
(Woh-der meeng-dzu shr De Mente)

What time does the coffee shop open?
Kafei dian jidian kaimen? 咖啡店几点开门？
(Kah-fay dee-an jee-dee-an kigh-mern)

Where is the bar?
Jiuba zai nali? 酒吧在哪里？
(Jeo-bah zigh nah-lee)

*Electrical voltage in China is 220, so American-made appliances designed for 110 volts do not work well. Newer hotels have outlets for both 220V and 110V. But if you are going to stay in older, out-of-the way hotels, you might want to take along a voltage converter.

How much is the room tax?
Fangjian shui duoshao? 房间税多少？
(Fahng-jee-an shway dwoh-shou)

Toilet / Restroom

As in English, there are several words for toilet in Chinese.

toilet	*cesuo (tser-swoh)*	厕所
restroom	*weishengjian (way-sherng-jee-an)*	卫生间
washroom	*xishou jian (she-show jee-an)*	洗手间
powder room	*huazhuang jian (hwah-jwahng jee-an)*	化装间
men's toilet	*nan cesuo (nahn tser-swoh)*	男厕所
women's toilet	*nu cesuo (noo tser-swoh)*	女厕所
toilet paper	*shou zhi (show jr)*	手纸

Where is the nearest toilet?
Zuijin-de cesuo zai nali? 最近的厕所在那里？
(Zway-jeen-der tser-swoh zigh nah-lee)

Is there a toilet on this floor?
Zhe yi ceng you cesuo ma? 这一层有厕所吗？
(Juh ee tserng you tser-swoh mah)

May I use the toilet?
Wo keyi yong cesuo ma? 我可以用厕所吗？
(Woh ker-ee yohng tser-swoh mah)

The Seasons

season	*jijie (jee-jeeh)* 季节
spring	*chunji (choon-jee)* 春季
springtime	*zai chuntian (zigh choon-tee-an)* 在春天
summer	*xiaji (she-ah-jee)* 夏季
summertime	*zai xiatian (zigh she-ah-tee-an)* 在夏天
fall	*qiuji (chew-jee)* 秋季
autumn	*qiutian (chew-tee-an)* 秋天
winter	*dongji (dohng-jee)* 冬季
wintertime	*zai dongji (zigh dohng-jee)* 在冬季

The Weather

weather	*tianqi* (tee-an-chee) 天气
weather forecast	*tianqi yubao* (teen-an-chee yuu-bow) 天气预报
wind	*feng* (ferng) 风
windy	*guafeng-de* (gwah-ferng-der) 刮风的
cloudy	*yin* (een) 阴
dust	*chentu* (churn-too) 尘土
cold	*leng* (lerng) 冷
coat	*shangyi* (shahng-ee) 上衣
hot	*re* (ruh) 热
humid	*chaoshi* (chow-shr) 潮湿
humidity	*shiqi* (shr-chee) 湿气
temperature	*qiwen* (chee-wern) 气温
rain	*yushui* (yuu-shway) 雨水
heavy rain	*da yu* (dah yuu) 大雨
typhoon	*taifeng* (tie-ferng) 台风
storm	*baofengyu* (bow-ferng-yuu) 暴风雨
raincoat	*yuyi* (yuu-ee) 雨衣
umbrella	*yusan* (yuu-sahn) 雨伞
snow	*xue* (shu-eh) 雪
ice	*bing* (beeng) 冰

It's hot!
Man re du! 蛮热的！
(Mahn ruh der)

It's cold!
Man leng de! 蛮冷的！
(Mahn lerng der)

It's raining.
Xia yu le. 下雨了。
(She-ah yuu ler)

It's snowing.
Xia xue le. 下雪了。
(She-ah shu-eh ler)

It's windy.
Feng da. 风大。
(Ferng dah)

The weather is beautiful.
Tianqi hao jile. 天气好极了。
(Tee-an-chee how jee-ler)

What is the weather going to be like tomorrow?
Mingtian tianqi zenme yang? 明天天气怎么样？
(Meeng-tee-an tee-an-chee zern-mer yahng)

Should we take our umbrellas?
Yao dai yusan ma? 要带雨伞吗？
(Yee-ow die yuu-sahn mah)

Eating

| Chinese food | *Zhong can (Johng tsahn)* 中餐 |
| Chinese restaurant | *Zhong canting (Johng tsahn-teeng)* 中餐厅 |

To specify a regional style of cooking, prefix the name to *shi (shr)*. Here are the four most famous styles:

Shanghai style	*Shanghai shi (Shahng-high shr)* 上海式
Szechuan style	*Sichuan shi (Suh-chwahn shr)* 四川式
Beijing style	*Beifang shi (Bay-fahng shr)* 北方式
Cantonese style	*Guangdong shi (Gwahng-dohng shr)* 广东式
Beijing dishes	*Beijing cai (Bay-jeeng tsigh)* 北京菜
Cantonese dishes	*Guangdong cai (Gwahng-dohng tsigh)* 广东菜
Szechuan dishes	*Sichuan cai (Suh-chwahn tsigh)* 四川菜
Shanghai dishes	*Shanghai cai (Shahn-high tsigh)* 上海菜
Chinese appetizers	*Youming Zhongguo kaiwei xiaocai (You-meeng Johng-gwoh kigh-way she-ow-tsigh)* 有名中国开胃小菜
restaurant	*fanguan (fahn-gwahn)* 饭馆
famous restaurant	*fan zhuang (fahn jwahng)* 饭庄
hotel restaurant	*fan dian (fahn dee-an)* 饭店
cafeteria	*can guan (tsahn gwahn)* 餐馆
snackbar	*xiaochi dian (she-ow-chr dee-an)* 小吃店
Chinese snackbar	*fengwei xiaochi (ferng-way she-ow-chr)* 风味小吃
American food	*Meiguo can (May-gwoh tsahn)* 美国餐
Western food	*Xi can (She tsahn)* 西餐

American-style breakfast
Meiguo zaocan 美国早餐
(May-gwoh zow-tsahn)

American-style sandwich
Meiguo sanmingzhi 美国三明治
(May-gwoh sahn-meeng-jr)

American-style dessert
Meiguo tianshi 美国甜食
(May-gwoh tee-an-shr)

Chinese-style breakfast
Zhongguo zaocan 中国早餐
(Johng-gwoh zow-tsahn)

Chinese-style dessert
Zhongguo tianshi 中国甜食
(Johng-gwoh tee-an-shr)

menu	*caidan (tsigh-dahn)* 菜单
English menu	*Yingyu caidan (Eeng-yuu tsigh-dahn)* 英语菜单
waiter	*fuwuyuan (foo-woo-ywahn)* 服务员
appetizers	*kaiweipin (kigh-way-peen)* 开胃品
fork	*chazi (chah-dzu)* 叉子
knife	*daozi (dow-dzu)* 刀子
spoon	*shaozi (shou-dzu)* 勺子
napkin	*canjin (tsahn-jeen)* 餐巾
rice, cooked	*mifan (me-fahn)* 米饭
soup	*tang (tahng)* 汤
steak	*niupai (new-pie)* 牛排

famous dim sum dishes
youming dian xin 有名点心
(you-meeng dee-an sheen)

famous fish dishes
youming yu cai 有名鱼菜
(you-meeng yuu tsigh)

famous pork dishes
youming rou cai 有名肉菜
(you-meeng roe tsigh)

famous vegetable dishes
youming shu cai 有名蔬菜
(you-meeng shoo tsigh)

seafood	*haiwei (high-way)*	海味
fruit	*shuiguo (shway-gwoh)*	水果
vegetables	*shucai (shoo-tsigh)*	蔬菜
chopsticks	*kuaizi (kwie-dzu)*	筷子
toothpick	*yaqian (yah-chee-an)*	牙签
delicious	*haochi (how-chr)*	好吃

I would like to make reservations for dinner this evening.
Wo yao ding jintian de wanfan. 我要定今天的晚饭。
(Woh yee-ow deeng jeen-teen-an der wahn-fahn)

There will be three people.
Wo-men you san-ge ren. 我们有三个人。
(Woh-mern you sahn-guh wren)

We want to go to a Peking duck restaurant.
Wo-men xiang qu yige Beijing kaoya guan.
(Woh-mern she-ahng chwee ee-guh Bay-jeeng kow-yah gwahn)
我们想去一个北京烤鸭馆。

I'm hungry.
Wo e le. 我饿了。
(Woh eh ler)

I'm thirsty.
Wo ke le. 我渴了。
(Woh kuh ler)

Please bring us menus.
Qing gei wo-men caidan. 请给我们菜单。
(Cheeng gay woh-mern tsigh-dahn)

Please bring us wet towels.
Qing gei wo-men shi maojin. 请给我们湿毛巾。
(Cheeng gay woh-mern shr mao-jeen)

Please bring us hot towels.
Qing gei wo-men re maojin. 请给我们热毛巾。
(Cheeng gay woh-mern ruh mao-jeen)

It tastes good!
Kekou! 可口!
(Ker-koe)

No more, thanks!
Gou-le, xiexie! 够了，谢谢!
(Go-ler, she-eh-she-eh)

Drinking

drink (noun)   *yinliao (een-lee-ow)* 饮料
to drink (verb)   *he (her)* 喝
bar   *jiuba (jeo-bah)* 酒吧
nightclub   *ye zonghui (yeh johng-hway)* 夜总会

Is there a cover charge?
You ruchang feiyong ma? 有入场费用吗？
(You roo-chahng fay-yohng mah)

How much is the cover charge?
Ruchang duoshao qian? 入场多少钱？
(Roo-chahng dwoh-shou chee-an)

Would you like to dance?
Ni xiang gen wo tiaowu ma? 你想跟我跳舞吗？
(Nee shee-ahng gurn woh tee-ow-woh mah)

karaoke lounge   *kala-OK ting (kah-lah-oh-kay teeng)*
卡拉 OK 厅

How much (do you charge) per hour?
Yi xiaoshi duoshao qian? 一小时多少钱？
(Ee she-ow-shr dwoh-shou chee-an?)

Do you have Western songs?
Ni-men you Xiyang ge mah? 你们有西洋歌吗？
(Nee-mern you She-yahng guh mah)

café	*leng yindian (lerng een-deen-an)* 冷饮店
coffee	*kafei (kah-fay)* 咖啡
coffee with cream	*kafei, jia niunai (kah-fay, jee-ah new-nigh)* 咖啡，加牛奶
coffee shop	*kafei ting (kah-fay teeng)* 咖啡厅
teahouse	*chaguan (chah-gwahn)* 茶馆
maotai	*(mao-tie)* 茅台
(China's famous banquet and toast drink)	
Cheers!	*Ganbei! (Gahn-bay)* 干杯！
wine	*putaojiu (poo-tou-jeo)* 葡萄酒
rice wine	*shaoxing jiu (shou-sheeng jeo)* 绍兴酒
beer (Western)	*pijiu (pee-jeo)* 啤酒
draft beer	*zha pi (jah pee)* 喳啤
cold drink	*leng yin (lerng een)* 冷饮
water	*shui (shway)* 水
ice water	*bing shui (beeng shway)* 冰水
hot water	*kai shui (kigh shway)* 开水
mineral water	*kuangquan shui (kwahng-chwahn shway)* 矿泉水
orange juice	*juzi shui (jwee-dzu shway)* 橘子水
hangover	*zui (zway)* 醉
milk	*niunai (neo-nigh)* 牛奶
tea (black)	*hong cha (hohng chah)* 红茶
jasmine tea	*molihua cha (mwo-lee-hwah chah)* 茉莉花茶

I'm thirsty.
Wo kele. 我渴了。
(Woh ker-ler)

Black tea, please.
Qing gei wo hong cha. 请给我红茶。
(Cheeng gay woh hohng chah)

Please bring me a bottle of beer.
Qing gei wo lai yi ping pijiu. 请给我来一瓶啤酒。
(Cheen gay woh lie ee-peeng pee-jeo)

Please bring me a glass of red wine.
Qing gei wo lai yi-bei hong putao jiu.
(Cheeng gay woh lie ee-bay hohng poo-tao-jeo)
请给我来一杯红葡萄酒。

Please bring us some peanuts.
Qing gei wo-men lai dian huashengmi.
(Cheeng gay woh-mern lie dee-an hwah-sherng-me)
请给我们来点花生米。

Paying Bills

bill, check   *zhangdan (jahng-dahn)* 帐单
separate checks   *fenkai suan (fern-kigh swahn)* 分开算
receipt   *shouju (show-jwee)* 收据
credit card   *shinyong ka (sheen-yohng kah)* 信用卡

The bill, please.
Qing suan zhang. 请算帐。
(Cheeng swahn jahng)

Do you accept credit cards?
Shingyong ka keyi ma? 信用卡可以吗？
(Sheeng-yohng kah ker-ee mah)

Separate checks, please.
Qing fenkai suan. 请分开算。
(Cheeng fern-kigh swahn)

Telephone / Email

telephone   *dianhua (dee-an hwah)* 电话
public telephone   *gongyong dianhua (gohng-yohng dee-an-hwah)* 公用电话
inhouse phone   *neixian dianhua (nay-shee-an dee-an-hwah)* 内线电话
cell phone   *shou ji (show jee)* 手机
telephone number   *dianhua haoma (dee-an-hwah how-mah)* 电话号码
make a phone call   *da dianhua (dah dee-an-hwah)* 打电话
hello!   *wei! (way)* 喂！
goodbye   *zaijian (zigh-jee-an)* 再见
local call   *bendi dianhua (bern-dee dee-an-hwah)* 本地电话
domestic call   *guonei dianhua (gwoh-nay dee-an-hwah)* 国内电话
long-distance call   *changtu dianhua (chahng-too dee-an-hwah)* 长途电话
international call   *guowai dianhua (gwoh-wigh dee-an-hwah)* 国外电话
collect call   *shuohuaren fufei dianhua (shwo-hwah-wren foo-fay dee-an-hwah)* 说话人付费电话
United States   *Meiguo (May-gwoh)* 美国
email   *dianzi youjian (dee-an-dzu you-jeen-an)* 电子邮件
internet   *yingtewang (eeng-ter-wahng)* 应特网
internet café   *yingtewang kafeiting (eeng-ter-wahng kah-fay teeng)* 应特网咖啡厅

I want to make (a/an) _____ call.
Wo yao da yi-ge _____ dianhua. 我要打一个 _____ 电话。
(Woh yee-ow dah ee-guh _____ dee-an-hwah)

I want to make an international call.
Wo yao da yige guoji changtu dianhua.
(Woh yee-ow dah ee-guh gwoh-jee chahng-too dee-an hwah)
我要打一个国际长途电话。

May I use your phone?
Wo keyi yong ni de dianhua ma? 我可以用你的电话吗？
(Woh ker-ee yohng nee der dee-an-hwah mah)

Can I dial direct?
Neng zhijie bo ma? 能直接拨吗？
(Nerng jr-jee-eh bwo mah)

International direct dialing
Guoji zhijie changtu bohao 国际直接长途拨号
(Gwoh-jee jr-jee-eh chahng-too bwo-how)

May I use a computer?
Wo keyi yong diannao ma? 我可以用电脑吗？
(Woh ker-ee yohng dee-an-now mah)

I want to check my email.
Wo xiang cha wo-de dianzi youjian. 我想查我的电子邮件。
(Woh she-ahng chah woh-der dee-an-dzu you-jee-an)

Where can I rent a cell phone?
Zai nali keyi zudao shou ji? 在那里可以租到手机？
(Zigh nah-lee ker-ee joo-dow show jee)

Shopping

shop / store	*shangdian (shahng-dee-an)* 商店
shopping	*mai dongxi (my dohng-she)* 买东西
shopping center	*shang chang (shahng-chahng)* 商场
	shangpin bu (shahng-peen boo) 商品铺
shopping street	*gouwu jie (go-woo jee-eh)* 购物街
department store	*baihuo shangdian (by-hwoh shahng dee-an)* 百货商店
souvenir / gift shop	*luyou jinianpin shangdian (lwee-you jee-nee-an-peen shahng dee-an)* 旅游纪念品商店
bookstore	*shu dian (shoo dee-an)* 书店
buy	*mai (my)* 买
calling female clerk	*xiao jie (she-ow jee-eh)* 小姐
calling any clerk	*shifu (shr-foo)* 师傅
antique	*gudong (goo-dohng)* 古董
chinaware	*ciqi (tsu-chee)* 瓷器
handicrafts	*shougongyi pin (show-gohng-ee peen)* 手工艺品
jade carving	*yudiao (yuu-dee-ow)* 玉雕
jewelry	*zhubao (joo-bow)* 珠宝
silk	*sichou (tsuh-choe)* 丝绸

I want to buy _____
Xiang mai _____ 想买 _____
(She-ahng my _____)

Please show me _____

Qing gei wo kankan _____ 请给我看看 _____

(*Cheeng gay woh kahn-kahn* _____)

How much is it?

Duoshao qian? 多少钱？

(*Dwoh-shou chee-an*)

Too expensive.

Tai gui-le 太贵了。

(*Tie gway-ler*)

It doesn't fit me.

Bu heshen. 不合身。

(*Boo her-shern*)

This is the wrong size.

Zhe daxiao bu-dui. 这大小不对。

(*Juh dah-she-ow boo-dway*)

Business

business	*shengyi (sherng-ee)* 生意
businessperson	*shangren (shahng-wren)* 商人
office	*bangongshi (bahn-gohng-shr)* 办公室
office building	*bangong lou (bahn-gohng low)* 办公楼
address	*dizhi (dee-jr)* 地址
office hours	*bangongshi jian (bahn-gohng-shr jee-an)* 办公时间
company	*gongsi (gohng-suh)* 公司
appointment	*yuehui (yu-eh hway)* 约会

Where is your office?
Nali shi ni-de bangong shi? 那里是你的办公室？
(Nah-lee shr nee-der bahn-gohng shr)

What is your address?
Ni-de zhu zhi shi? 你的住址是？
(Nee-der joo jr shr)

I have an appointment with Mr. Lee.
Wo gen Lee Xiansheng you yuehui.
(Woh gurn Lee She-an-sherng you yuu-eh-hway)
我跟李先生有约会。

Post Office

post office	*you ju (you jwee)* 邮局
mail	*youjian (you-jee-an)* 邮件
airmail	*hangkong (hahng-kohng)* 航空
surface mail	*ping you (peeng you)* 平邮
express mail	*kuaidi youjian (kwie-dee you-jee-an)* 快递邮件
registered letter	*guahao xin (gwah-how sheen)* 挂号信
parcel, package	*baoguo (bow-gwoh)* 包裹
postage stamp	*you piao (you pee-ow)* 邮票
special delivery	*xianshi zhuansong (shee-an-shr jwahn-sohng)* 现时专送

Where is the nearest post office?
Zuijin-de you ju zai nali? 最近的邮局在那里？
(Zway-jeen-der you jwee zigh nah-lee)

An airmail stamp, please.
Mai hangkong youpiao. 买航空邮票。
(My hahng-kohng you-pee-ow)

Health / Help

help!   *jiu ming!* (*jeo meeng*) 救命！

Please help me!
Qing kuai lai bang wo! 请快来帮我！
(*Cheeng kwie lie bahng woh*)

sick	*shengbing-le* (*sherng-beeng-ler*) 生病了
doctor	*daifu* (*die-foo*) 大夫
	yisheng (*ee-sherng*) 医生
ambulance	*jiuhuche* (*jeo-hoo-cher*) 救护车
hospital	*yiyuan* (*ee-ywahn*) 医院
injury	*shang* (*shahng*) 伤
pain / hurt	*tong* (*tohng*) 痛 / *teng* (*terng*) 疼
emergency room	*jizhen shi* (*jee-jern shr*) 急诊室
fever	*fashao-le* (*fah-shou-ler*) 发烧了
temperature	*tiwen* (*tee-wern*) 体温
headache	*touteng* (*toe-terng*) 头疼
a cold	*shangfeng-le* (*shahng-ferng-ler*) 伤风了
stomachache	*duzi teng* (*doo-dzu terng*) 肚子疼
diarrhea	*xieduzi* (*she-eh-doo-dzu*) 泻肚子
dysentery	*youliji* (*you-lee-jee*) 游痢疾
food poisoning	*shiwu zhongdu* (*shr-woo johng-doo*) 食物中毒
vomit	*outu* (*oh-too*) 呕吐
toothache	*ya teng* (*yah terng*) 牙疼
dentist	*yayi* (*yah-ee*) 牙医
	yake yisheng (*yak-ker ee-sherng*) 牙科医生
allergy	*guomin* (*gwoh-meen*) 过敏
high blood pressure	*gao xueya* (*gow shu-eh-yah*) 高血压

eyes	*yan (yahn)* 眼
eyeglasses	*yanjing (yahn-jeeng)* 眼镜
health insurance	*jiankang baoxian (jee-an-kahng bow-shee-an)* 健康保险

I'm sick.
Wo bing le. 我病了。
(Woh beeng ler)

It hurts here.
Zheli tong. 这里痛。
(Juh-lee tohng)

I have a toothache.
Wo yatong. 我牙痛。
(Woh yah-tohng)

I have a headache.
Wo toutong. 我头痛。
(Woh toe-tohng)

I have a stomachache.
Wo weitong. 我胃痛。
(Woh way-tohng)

I feel dizzy.
Wo touyun. 我头晕。
(Woh toe-ywun)

Is there a drugstore in the hotel?
Luguan you yaofang ma? 旅馆有药房吗？
(Lwee-gwahn you yee-ow-fahng mah)

What time does the drugstore open?
Yaofang jidian kai? 药房几点开？
(Yee-ow-fahng jee-dee-an kigh)

I'm not feeling well.
Wo youdian bu shufu. 我有点不舒服。
(Woh you-dee-an boo shoo-foo)

I've caught a cold.
Wo ganmao le. 我感冒了。
(Woh gahn-mao ler)

I'm sick, please call a doctor.
Wo sheng bing-le, qing jiao yisheng.
(Woh sherng beeng-ler, cheeng jee-ow ee-sherng)
我生病了，请叫医生。

Is there a doctor who speaks English?
You neng shuo Yinyu de yisheng ma?
(You nerng shwo Eenyuu der ee-sherng mah)
有能说英语的医生吗？

I am allergic to _____ .
Wo dui _____ guomin. 我对 _____ 过敏。
(Woh dwee _____ gwoh-meen)

There's been an accident!
Chushi-le! 出事了！
(Choo-shr-ler)

Please call an ambulance.
Qing jiao jiuhuche. 请叫救护车。
(Cheeng jee-ow jeo-hoo-cher)

I lost my glasses.
Wo-de yanjing diu-le. 我的眼镜丢了。
(*Woh-der yahn-jeeng deo-ler*)

police   *jingcha* (*jeeng-chah*) 警察
police station   *jingcha ju* (*jeeng-chah jwee*) 警察局
                       gongan ju (*gohng-ahn jwee*) 公安局

Please call the police.
Qing jiao jingcha. 请叫警察。
(*Cheeng jee-ow jeeng-cha*)

I lost my passport.
Wo de huzhao bu jian le. 我的护照不见了。
(*Woh der hoo-jow boo jee-an ler*)

I've lost my suitcase.
Wo diu le tibao. 我丢了提包。
(*Woh deo ler tee-bow*)

Can you please help me?
Ni keyi bang wo ma? 你可以帮我吗？
(*Nee ker-ee bahng woh mah*)

Do you speak English?
Ni neng shuo Yingyu ma? 你能说英语吗？
(*Nee nerng shwo Eeng-yuu mah*)

embassy   *dashiguan* (*dah-shr-gwahn*) 大使馆
American Embassy   *Meiguo Dashiguan* (*May-gwoh Dah-shr-gwahn*) 美国大使馆

Sightseeing

sightseeing	*guanguang (gwahn-gwahng)* 观光	
	youlan (you-lahn) 游览	
tourist guide	*daoyou (dow-you)* 导游	
tourist bus	*luyou che (lwee-you cher)* 旅游车	
tourist sites	*luyou dian (lwee-you dee-an)* 旅游点	
tourist map	*luyou ditu (lwee-you dee-too)* 旅游地图	
city map	*shiqu ditu (shr-chwee dee-too)* 市区地图	
local/area map	*dangdi ditu (dahng-dee dee-too)* 当地 地图	
Tiananmen Square	*Tiananmen guangchang (Tee-an-ahn-mern gwahng-chahng)* 天安门广场	
Buddhist temple	*si yuan (suh ywahn)* 寺院	
	miao (mee-ow) 庙	
Taoist temple	*guan (gwahn)* 观	
art gallery	*meishu guan (may-shoo gwahn)* 美术馆	
museum	*bowuguan (bwo-woo-gwahn)* 博物馆	
Summer Palace	*Yiheyuan (Ee-her-ywahn)* 颐和园	

I want an English speaking tourist guide.
Wo yao yi-ge Yinguo daoyou. 我要一个英国导游。
(Woh yee-ow ee-guh Eeng-gwoh dow-you)

What is the rate per hour?
Mei xiaoshi duoshao qian? 每小时多少钱？
(May she-ow-shr dwoh-shou chee-an)

Is it all right to take photographs?
Rang paizhao ma? 让拍照吗？
(Rahng pie-jow mah)

Please (go) take me to the Ming Tombs.
Qing qu Shisanling. 请去十三陵。
(Cheeng chwee Shr-sahn-leeng)

Please take us to the Great Wall.
Qing qu Chang Cheng. 请去长城。
(Cheeng chwee Chahng Churng)

Barber Shop / Beauty Salon

barber shop	*lifa dian (lee-fah dee-an)*	理发店
haircut	*lifa (lee-fah)*	理发
beauty salon	*falang (fah-lahng)*	发廊
shampoo	*xi tou (she toe)*	洗头
permanent	*tang toufa (tahng toe-fah)*	烫头发
hair wash	*xifa (she-fah)*	洗发
hair curl	*juanfa (jwen-fah)*	卷发
manicure	*xiu zhijia (shew jr-jee-ah)*	修指甲
pedicure	*xiu jiao zhijia (shew jee-ow jr-jee-ah)* 修脚指甲	

I'd like to make an appointment for this afternoon.
Wo xiang yuding jintian xiawu. 我想预定今天下午。
(Woh she-ahng yuu-deeng jeen-tee-an she-ah-woo)

Please give me a haircut.
Qing wei wo lifa. 请为我理发。
(Cheeng way woh lee-fah)

Please give me a shampoo.
Qing wei wo xitou. 请为我洗头。
(Cheeng way woh she-toe)

I'd like a shave, please.
Wo yao gua lian. 我要刮脸。
(Woh yee-ow gwah lee-an)

I'd like a massage, please.
Wo yao anmo. 我要按摩。
(Woh yee-ow ahn-mwo)

Measurements

(China uses the metric system)

centimeter	*limi (lee-me)*	厘米
meter	*mi (me)*	米
kilometer	*gongli (gohng-lee)*	公里
gram	*gongke (gohng-ker)*	公克
kilogram	*gongjin (gohng-jeen)*	公斤
liter	*sheng (sherng)*	升
gallon	*jialun (jah-loon)*	加仑
hectare (2.47 acres)	*gongqing (gohng-cheeng)*	公顷
foot	*yingchi (eeng-chr)*	英尺
inch	*yingcun (eeng-tsoon)*	英寸
mile	*yingli (eeng-lee)*	英里
yard	*ma (mah)*	码

Personal Titles

Mr.	*Xiansheng (She-ahn sherng)*	先生
Mrs.	*Taitai (Tie-tie)*	太太
	Furen (Foo-wren)	夫人
Miss / Ms	*Nushi (Nwee-shr)*	女士

Academic Titles

chancellor, president	*xiaozhang (she-ow-jahng)*	校长
department head	*xi zhuren (she joo-wren)*	系主任
professor	*jiaoshou (jee-ow-show)*	教授
teacher	*laoshi (lao-shr)*	老师
	jiaoshi (jee-ow-shr)	教师
student	*xuesheng (shu-eh-sherng)*	学生

Business & Professional Titles

accountant	*kuaijishi (kwie-jee-shr)*	会计师
attorney	*lushi (lwee-shr)*	律师
banker	*yinhangjia (een-hahng-jee-ah)*	银行家
businessperson	*shangren (shahng-wren)*	商人
computer specialist	*diannao zhuanjia (dee-an-now jwahn-jee-ah)*	电脑专家
consultant	*guwen (goo-wern)*	顾问
doctor	*yisheng (ee-sherng)*	医生
driver	*siji (suh-jee)*	司机
editor	*bianji (bee-an-jee)*	编辑
engineer	*gongchengshi (gohng-churng-shr)*	工程师
entertainer	*biaoyanzhe (bee-ow-yahn-juh)*	表演者
factory manager	*changzhang (chahng-jahng)*	厂长
farmer	*nongfu (nohng-foo)*	农夫
general manager	*zong jingli (zohng jeeng-lee)*	总经理
government official	*guan (gwahn)*	官
government worker	*zhengfu ren yuan (jehng foo wren ywahn)*	政府人员

governor	*shengzhang (sherng-jahng)* 省长	
guide	*daoyou (dow-you)* 导游	
journalist	*jizhe (jee-juh)* 记者	
laborer	*gongren (gohng-wren)* 工人	
librarian	*tushuguanliyuan (too-shoo-gwahn-lee-ywahn)* 图书管理员	
manager	*jingli (jeeng-lee)* 经理	
mayor	*shizhang (shr-jahng)* 市长	
mechanic	*jigong (jee-gohng)* 技工	
musician	*yinyuejia (een-yu-eh-jee-ah)* 音乐家	
nurse	*hushi (hoo-shr)* 护士	
office worker	*zhiyuan (jr-ywahn)* 职员	
Ph.D, Dr.	*boshi (bwo-shr)* 博士	
photographer	*sheyingshi (sher-eeng-shr)* 摄影师	
professor	*jiaoshou (jee-ow-show)* 教授	
scientist	*kexuejia (ker-shu-eh-jee-ah)* 科学家	
secretary	*mishu (me-shoo)* 秘书	
sportsperson	*yundongyuan (ywun-dohng-ywahn)* 运动员	
student	*xuesheng (shu-eh-sherng)* 学生	
teacher	*laoshi (lao-shr)* 老师	
technician	*jishuyuan (jee-shoo-ywahn)* 技术员	
tourist	*luke (lwee-ker)* 旅客	
translator	*fanyi (fahn-ee)* 翻译	
travel agent	*luxing yuan (lwee-sheeng ywahn)* 旅行员	
writer	*zuojia (zwoh-jee-ah)* 作家	

*One of the traditional courtesies used in China when addressing older people is to put the word *lao (lou)* in front of their family name, as in *Lao Chang*. *Lao* means "old" and when used in this way it has the connotation of "honored older person."

Homes

home	*jia (jee-ah)* 家
house	*fangzi (fahng-dzu)* 房子
apartment	*danyuanfang (dahn-ywahn-fahng)* 单元房
invitation	*qingjian (cheeng-jee-an)* 请東
invite	*yaoqing (yee-ow-cheeng)* 邀请
kitchen	*chufang (choo-fahng)* 厨房
dining room	*can shi (tsahn shr)* 餐室
bathroom	*yushi (yuu-shr)* 浴室

Please give me your address.
Qing gaosu wo ni de dizhi. 请告诉我你的地址。
(Cheeng gow-soo woh nee der dee-jr)

May I come in?
Neng jinlai ma? 能进来吗？
(Nerng jeen-lie mah)

The food was delicious.
Fan hen xiang. 饭很香。
(Fahn hern she-ahng)

Thank you for a wonderful evening.
Xiexie jin wan hen gaoxin. 谢谢今晚很高兴。
(She-eh-she-eh jeen wahn hern gow-sheen)

PART 2

The Cardinal Numbers

Numbers are one of the most important parts of human speech and communication. Like English and other languages, numbers in Chinese are based on original terms from one through ten, and then combinations of these ten terms.

0   *ling (leeng)* 零
1   *yi (ee)** 一

*The pronunciation of yi changes to *yao (yee-ow)* when used in higher numbers. For example, 118 is *yao yao ba (yee-ow yee-ow bah)*.

2   *er (urr)* 二; also *liang (lee-ahng)* 两
3   *san (sahn)* 三
4   *si (suh)* 四
5   *wu (woo)* 五
6   *liu (leo)* 六
7   *qi (chee)* 七
8   *ba (bah)* 八
9   *jiu (jeo)* 九
10   *shi (shr)* 十

As noted, from 10 on, the numbers are combinations of the first ten numbers. Eleven is 10 and 1, 12 is 10 and 2, etc. Twenty is 2–10; 30 is 3–10, and so on.

11   *shiyi (shr-ee)* 十一
12   *shier (shr-urr)* 十二

13	*shisan (shr-sahn)* 十三
14	*shisi (shr-suh)* 十四
15	*shiwu (shr-woo)* 十五
16	*shiliu (shr-leo)* 十六
17	*shiqi (shr-chee)* 十七
18	*shiba (shr-bah)* 十八
19	*shijiu (shr-jeo)* 十九
20	*ershi (urr-shr)* 二十
21	*ershiyi (urr-shr-ee)* 二十一
22	*ershier (urr-shr-urr)* 二十二
23	*ershisan (urr-shr-sahn)* 二十三
24	*ershisi (urr-shr-suh* 二十四
25	*ershiwu (urr-shr-woo)* 二十五
26	*ershiliu (urr-shr-leo)* 二十六
27	*ershiqi (urr-shr-chee)* 二十七
28	*ershiba (urr-shr-bah)* 二十八
29	*ershijiu (urr-shr-jeo)* 二十九
30	*sanshi (sahn-shr)* 三十
31	*sanshiyi (sahn-shr-ee)* 三十一
32	*sanshier (sahn-shr-urr)* 三十二
33	*sanshisan (sahn-shr-sahn)* 三十三
34	*sanshisi (sahn-shr-suh* 三十四
35	*sanshiwu (sahn-shr-woo)* 三十五
36	*sanshiliu (sahn-shr-leo)* 三十六
37	*sanshiqi (sahn-shr-chee)* 三十七
38	*sanshiba (sahn-shr-bah)* 三十八
39	*sanshijiu (sahn-shr-jeo)* 三十九
40	*sishi (suh-shr)* 四十
41	*sishiyi (suh-shr-ee)* 四十一
50	*wushi (woo-shr)* 五十
60	*liushi (leo-shr)* 六十
70	*qishi (chee-shr)* 七十
80	*bashi (bah-shr)* 八十

| 90 | *jiushi (jeo-shr)* 九十 |
| 100 | *yibai (ee-by)** 一百 |

---

*bai is the designator for 100

101	*yibailingyi (ee-by-leeng-ee)* 一百零一
102	*yibailinger (ee-by-leeng-urr)* 一百零二
103	*yibailingsan (ee-by-leeng-sahn)* 一百零三
104	*yibailingsi (ee-by-leeng-suh)* 一百零四
105	*yibailingwu (ee-by-leeng-woo)* 一百零五
106	*yibailingliu (ee-by-leeng-leo)* 一百零六
107	*yibailingqi (ee-by-leeng-chee)* 一百零七
108	*yibailingba (ee-by-leeng-bah)* 一百零八
109	*yibailingjiu (ee-by-leeng-jeo)* 一百零九

110	*yibaiyishi (ee-by-ee-shr)* 一百一十
120	*yibaiershi (ee-by-urr-shr)* 一百二十
130	*yibaisanshi (ee-by-sahn-shr)* 一百三十
140	*yibaisishi (ee-by-suh-shr)* 一百四十
150	*yibaiwushi (ee-by-woo-shr)* 一百五十
175	*yibaiqishiwu (ee-by-chee-shr-woo)* 一百七十五

200	*erbai (urr-by)* 二百
201	*erbailingyi (urr-by-leeng-ee)* 二百零一
300	*sanbai (sahn-by)* 三百
400	*sibai (suh-by)* 四百
500	*wubai (woo-by)* 五百
600	*liubai (leo-by)* 六百
700	*qibai (chee-by)* 七百
800	*babai (bah-by)* 八百
900	*jiubai (jeo-by)* 九百
1,000	*yiqian** 一千

---

*Qian is the designator for 1,000.

1,500	*yiqianwubai* (ee-chee-an-woo-by) 一千五百
2,000	*liangqian* (lee-ahng-chee-an) 两千
2,700	*liangquanqibai* (lee-ahng-chee-an-chee-by) 两千七百
3,000	*sanqian* (sahn-chee-an) 三千
4,000	*siqian* (suh-chee-an) · 四千
5,000	*wuqian* (woo-chee-an) 五千
10,000	*yiwan** (ee-wahn) 一万

---

* *Wan* is the designator for 10,000.

11,000	*yiwanyiqian* (ee-wahn-ee-chee-an) 一万一千
12,000	*yiwanliangqian* (ee-wahn-lee-ahng-chee-an) 一万两千
15,000	*yiwanwuqian* (ee-wahn-woo-chee-an) 一万五千
20,000	*erwan* (urr-wahn) 二万
30,000	*sanwan* (sahn-wahn) 三万
40,000	*siwan* (suh-wahn) 四万
50,000	*wuwan* (woo-wahn) 五万
80,000	*bawan* (bah-wahn) 八万
100,000	*shiwan* (shr-wahn) 十万
150,000	*shiwuwan* (shr-woo-wahn) 十五万
200,000	*ershiwan* (urr-shr-wahn) 二十万
300,000	*sanshiwan* (sahn-shr-wahn) 三十万
500,000	*wushiwan* (woo-shr-wahn) 五十万
1,000,000	*yibaiwan* (ee-by-wahn) 一百万

The Ordinal Numbers

The ordinal numbers are created by adding the prefix *di (dee)*
to the cardinal numbers.

1st	*diyi (dee-ee)*	第一
2nd	*dier (dee-urr)*	第二
3rd	*disan (dee-sahn)*	第三
4th	*disi (dee-suh)*	第四
5th	*diwu (dee-woo)*	第五
6th	*diliu (dee-leo)*	第六
7th	*diqi (dee-chee)*	第七
8th	*diba (dee-bah)*	第八
9th	*dijiu (dee-jeo)*	第九
10th	*dishi (dee-shr)*	第十
11th	*dishiyi (dee-shr-ee)*	第十一
12th	*dishier (dee-shr-urr)*	第十二
13th	*dishisan (dee-shr-sahn)*	第十三
14th	*dishisi (dee-shr-suh)*	第十四
15th	*dishiwu (dee-shr-woo)*	第十五
20th	*diershi (dee-urr-shr)*	第二十
30th	*disanshi (dee-sahn-shr)*	第三十
50th	*diwushi (dee-woo-shr)*	第五十
one half	*yi ban (ee-bahn)*	一半
one quarter	*si fen zhi yi (suh fern jr ee)*	四分之一

Counting Things

As mentioned earlier, the Chinese language uses special indicators, or "measure words," for counting things, based on what they are—people, flat things, round things, animals, fish, etc. There are over a dozen such terms, so keeping them straight, and using them properly, can be a problem for the beginner.

However, the most common of these indicators, *ge* (*guh*), can be used when you are uncertain about which one to use. The "measure words" go between the numbers and the nouns they apply to. Here is a list of the most common ones:

ben (*bern*), used when counting books.

ci (*tsu*), used when counting the number of times something occurs.

ke (*ker*), used when counting trees.

suo (*swoh*), used when counting buildings and houses.

tiao (*tee-ow*), used when counting large, long, slender objects like telephone poles.

zhi (*jr*), used when counting small, round objects like pencils and sticks.

zhang (*jahng*), used when counting flat things like pieces of paper.

wan (*wahn*), used when referring to bowls and things that come in bowls.

ping (*peeng*), used for counting bottles and bottled things.

kuai (*kwie*), used when referring to money.

ren (*wren*), used when counting people.

bei (*bay*), used for counting glasses of water, etc.

I have three books.
Wo you san-ben shu. 我有三本书。
(Woh you sahn-bern shoo)

Pleave give me one sheet of paper.
Qing gei wo yi-zhang zhi. 请给我一张纸。
(Cheeng gay woh ee-jahng jr)

Two glasses of water, please.
Qing gei wo liang-bei shui. 请给我两杯水。
(Cheeng gay woh lee-ahng-bay shway)

Counting People

person	*ren (wren)* 人
people	*renmin (wren-meen)* 人民

1 person	*yi-ge ren (ee-guh wren)* 一个人
2 persons	*liang-ge ren (lee-ahng-guh wren)* 两个人
3 persons	*san-ge ren (sahn-ge wren)* 三个人
4 persons	*si-ge ren (suh-guh wren)* 四个人
5 persons	*wu-ge ren (woo-guh wren)* 五个人
6 persons	*liu-ge ren (leo-guh wren)* 六个人
7 persons	*qi-ge ren (chee-guh wren)* 七个人
8 persons	*ba-ge ren (bah-guh wren)* 八个人
9 persons	*jiu-ge ren (jeo-guh wren)* 九个人
10 people	*shi-ge renmin (shr-guh wren-meen)* 十个人民

Counting Other Things

2 bottles of beer.
Liang-ping bijiu. 两瓶啤酒。
(Lee-ahng-peeng pee-jeo)

3 glasses of water.
San-bei shui. 三杯水。
(Sahn-bay shway)

2 hamburgers.
Liang-ge hanbaobao. 两个汉堡包。
(Lee-ahng-guh hahn-bow-bow)

1 book.
Yi-ben shu. 一本书。
(Ee-burn shoo)

2 sheets of paper.
Liang-zhang zhi. 两张纸。
(Lee-ahng-jahng jr)

May I have a pen, please?
Qing gei wo yi zhi bi. 请给我一支笔。
(Cheeng gay woh ee jr bee)

One hamburger, please.
Qing gei yi-ge hanbaobao. 请给一个汉堡包。
(Cheeng gay ee-guh hahn-bow-bow)

Telling Time

Telling time in Chinese is a combination of the appropriate number, plus the word *dian* (*dee-in*), which means something like "point of time" and in this usage is the equivalent of the English "o'clock." There is another word for "o'clock"—*zhong* (*johng*)—that is seldom used in ordinary conversation.

time (of day)	*shijian* (*shr-jee-an*) 时间
hour	*xiaoshi* (*she-ow-shr*) 小时
half an hour	*ban xiaoshi* (*bahn-she-ow-shr*) 半小时
minute	*fen* (*fern*) 分
a.m.	*shangwu* (*shahng-woo*) 上午
p.m.	*xiawu* (*she-ah-woo*) 下午

In China the 24-hour day is divided into four periods:

midnight to 6 a.m. (early morning)	*qingzao* (*cheeng-zow*) 清早
6 a.m. to noon (morning)	*zaoshang* (*zow-shahng*) 早上
noon to 6 p.m. (afternoon)	*xiawu* (*she-ah-woo*) 下午
6 p.m. to midnight (evening)	*wanshang* (*wahn-shahng*) 晚上

In designating the time period as well as the hour, both words precede the hour, as in the following examples.

1 a.m.	*qingzao yi dian* (*cheeng-zow ee dee-an*) 清早一点
8 a.m.	*zaoshang ba dian* (*zow-shahng bah dee-an*) 早上八点
1 p.m.	*xiawu yi dian* (*she-ah-woo ee dee-an*) 下午一点

8 p.m.	*wanshang ba dian (wahn-shahng bah dee-an)* 晚上八点
what time?	*ji dian? (jee dee-an)* 几点？
at / in	*zai (zigh)* 在
early	*zao (zow)* 早
late	*wan (wahn)* 晚
on time	*zhunshi (joon-shr)* 准时
in the morning	*zai zaoshang (zigh zow-shahng)* 在早上
in the afternoon	*zai xiawu (zigh she-ah-woo)* 在下午
in the evening	*zai wanshang (zigh wahn-shahng)* 在晚上
1 o'clock	*yi dian (ee dee-an)* 一点
1 a.m.	*qingzao yi dian (cheeng-zow ee-dee-an)* 清早一点
1:10	*yi dian shifen (ee dee-an shr fern)* 一点十分
1:30	*yi dian ban (ee dee-an bahn)* 一点半
2 o'clock	*liang dian (lee-ahng dee-an)* 两点
3 o'clock	*san dian (sahn dee-an)* 三点
2 a.m.	*qingzao liang dian (cheeng-zow lee-ahng dee-an)* 清早两点
2 p.m.	*xiawu liang dian (she-ah-woo lee-ahng dee-an)* 下午两点
2:30	*liang dian ban (lee-ahng dee-an bahn)* 两点半
3 o'clock	*san dian (sahn dee-an)* 三点
3 a.m.	*qingzao san dian (cheeng-zow sahn dee-an)* 清早三点
3 p.m.	*xiawu san dian (she-ah-woo sahn dee-an)* 下午三点
3:15	*san dian shiwufen (sahn dee-an shr-woo-fern)* 三点十五分 / 三点一刻
3:30	*san dian ban (sahn dee-an bahn)* 三点半
4 o'clock	*si dian (suh dee-an)* 四点

5 o'clock	*wu dian* (woo dee-an)	五点
6 o'clock	*liu dian* (leo dee-an)	六点
7 o'clock	*qi dian* (chee dee-an)	七点
8 o'clock	*ba dian* (bah dee-an)	八点
9 o'clock	*jiu dian* (jeo dee-an)	九点
10 o'clock	*shi dian* (shr dee-an)	十点
11 o'clock	*shiyi dian* (shr-ee dee-an)	十一点
12 o'clock	*shier dian* (shr-urr dee-an)	十二点
It is 6:30	*liu dian ban* (leo dee-an bahn)	
	六点半	
It is 12:30	*shier dian ban* (shr-urr dee-an bahn)	
	十二点半	

What time are we leaving?
Wo-men shenme shijian zou? 我们什么时间走？
(Woh-mern shern-mer shr-jee-an dzow)

What time does the bus leave?
Gonggong qiche ji dian likai? 公共汽车几点离开？
(Gohng-gohng chee-cher jee-dee-an lee-kigh)

What time is breakfast?
Zaocan shi ji dian? 早餐是几点？
(Zow-tsahn shr jee dee-an)

What times is lunch?
Wucan shi ji dian? 午餐是几点？
(Woo-tsahn shr jee dee-an)

What times is dinner?
Wancan shi ji dian? 晚餐是几点？
(Wahn-tsahn shr jee dee-an)

Days of the Week

The days of the week, from Monday through Saturday, consist of the "day designator" *xingqi (sheeng-chee)* plus the numbers one through six. Sunday consists of the "day designator" plus the word for "day."

Monday	*Xingqiyi (Sheeng-chee-ee)* 星期一
Tuesday	*Xingqier (Sheeng-chee-urr)* 星期二
Wednesday	*Xingqisan (Sheeng-chee-sahn)* 星期三
Thursday	*Xingqisi (Sheeng-chee-suh)* 星期四
Friday	*Xingqiwu (Sheeng-chee-woo)* 星期五
Saturday	*Xingqiliu (Sheeng-chee-leo)* 星期六
Sunday	*Xingqitian (Sheeng-chee-tee-an)* 星期天

today	*jintian (jeen-tee-an)* 今天
tomorrow	*mingtian (meeng-tee-an)* 明天
day after tomorrow	*hou tian (hoe tee-an)* 后天
yesterday	*zuotian (zwaw-tee-an)* 昨天
day before yesterday	*qian tian (chee-an tee-an)* 前天
in the morning	*zai zaoshang (zigh zow-shahng)* 在早上
in the afternoon	*zai xiawu (zigh she-ah-woo)* 在下午
in the eventing	*zai wanshang (zigh wahn-shahng)* 在晚上
early	*zao (zow)* 早
late	*wan (wahn)* 晚
on time	*zhunshi (joon-shr)* 准时

Counting Days

1 day	*yi tian (ee tee-an)*	一天
2 days	*liang tian (lee-ahng tee-an)*	两天
3 days	*san tian (sahn tee-an)*	三天
4 days	*si tian (suh tee-an)*	四天
5 days	*wu tian (woo tee-an)*	五天
6 days	*liu tian (leo tee-an)*	六天
7 days	*qi tian (chee tee-an)*	七天
8 days	*ba tian (bah tee-an)*	八天
9 days	*jiu tian (jew tee-an)*	九天
10 days	*shi tian (shr tee-an)*	十天
21 days	*ershiyi tian (urr-shr-ee tee-an)*	二十一天

What day is today?
Jintian shi xingqi ji? 今天是星期几？
(Jeen-tee-an shr sheeng-chee jee)

Today is Monday.
Jintian shi Xingqiyi. 今天是星期一。
(Jeen-tee-an shr Sheeng-chee-ee)

Weeks

week	*xingqi (sheeng-chee)* 星期
this week	*zhei-ge xingqi (jay-guh sheeng-chee)* 这个星期
last week	*shang-ge xingqi (shahng-guh sheeng-chee)* 上个星期
next week	*xia-ge xingqi (she-ah sheeng-chee)* 下个星期
weekend	*zhoumo (joe-mwo)* 周末
week after next	*xiaxia-ge xingqi (she-ah-she-ah-guh sheeng-chee)* 下下个星期

Counting Weeks

1 week	*yi xingqi (ee sheeng-chee)* 一星期
2 weeks	*er xingqi (urr sheeng-chee)* 二星期
3 weeks	*san xingqi (sahn sheeng-chee)* 三星期
4 weeks	*si xingqi (suh sheeng-chee)* 四星期
5 weeks	*wu xingqi (woo sheeng-chee)* 五星期
6 weeks	*liu xingqi (leo sheeng-chee)* 六星期
7 weeks	*qi xingqi (chee sheeng-chee)* 七星期
8 weeks	*ba xingqi (bah sheeng-chee)* 八星期

I will be in China for 2 weeks.
Wo jiang zai Zongguo dai liang-ge duo xingqi.
(Woh jee-ahng zigh Johng-gwoh die lee-ahng-guh dwoh sheeng-chee)
我将在中国待两个多星期。

The Months

The Chinese word for month is **yue** *(yuu-eh)*. **Yue** is used when naming or listing the months, and **ri** *(rr)* is used when giving dates. The names of the months consist of the appropriate number plus **yue**—in other words, **yi** (one) plus **yue** (month) equals January.

January	*Yiyue (Ee-yuu-eh)*	一月
February	*Eryue (Urr-yuu-eh)*	二月
March	*Sanyue (Sahn-yuu-eh)*	三月
April	*Siyue (Suh-yuu-eh)*	四月
May	*Wuyue (Woo-yuu-eh)*	五月
June	*Liuyue (Leo-yuu-eh)*	六月
July	*Qiyue (Chee-yuu-eh)*	七月
August	*Bayue (Bah-yuu-eh)*	八月
September	*Jiuyue (Jeo-yuu-eh)*	九月
October	*Shiyue (Shr-yuu-eh)*	十月
November	*Shiyiyue (Shr-ee-yuu-eh)*	十一月
December	*Shieryue (Shr-urr-yuu-eh)*	十二月

this month	*zhei-ge yue (jay-guh yuu-eh)*	这个月
next month	*xia-ge yue (she-ah-guh yuu-eh)*	下个月
last month	*shang-ge yue (shahng-guh yuu-eh)*	上个月
month after next	*xiaxia-ge yue (she-ah-she-ah-guh yuu-eh)*	下下个月
monthly	*mei-ge yue (may-guh yuu-eh)*	每个月

To enumerate months, just add the prefix *ge (guh)* to *yue*, the word for month, and put the appropriate number in front of the word:

1 month	*yi geyue (ee guh-yuu-eh)* 一个月
2 months	*liang geyue (lee-ang guh-yuu-eh)* 两个月
5 months	*wu geyue (woo guh-yuu-eh)* 五个月
6 months	*liu geyue (leo guh-yuu-eh)* 六个月
12 months	*shier geyue (shr-urr guh-yuu-eh)* 十二个月
every month	*mei-ge yue (may-guh yuu-eh)* 每个月
a few months	*ji-ge yue (jee-guh yuu-eh)* 几个月

The Years

The Chinese word for year is *nian (nee-an)*.

this year	*jin nian (jeen nee-an)* 今年
next year	*ming nian (meeng nee-an)* 明年
last year	*qu nian (chwee nee-an)* 去年
every year	*mei nian (may nee-an)* 每年
one year	*yi nian (ee nee-an)* 一年
two years	*liang nian (lee-ahng nee-an)* 两年
three years	*san nian (sahn nee-an)* 三年
four years	*si nian (suh nee-an)* 四年
five years	*wu nian (woo nee-an)* 五年
Happy New Year!	*Xin Nian Hao! (Sheen Nee-an How)* 新年好！
New Year's Day	*Yuan Dan (Ywahn Dahn)* 元旦

Giving Dates

In Chinese, dates are given with the year (*nian* / *nee-an*) first, the month (*yue* / *yu-eh*) second, and the day (*hao* / *how*) last. Example: **2010, January, 1.**

> *Erlingyiling nian yi yue yi hao*
> *(Urr-leeng-ee-leeng nee-an, ee-yu-eh ee how)*

In the days of the month, *hao* (*how*) may be used in place of *ri* (*rr*)...and it is a lot easier to pronounce!

1st of the month	*yiri (ee-rr)*	一日
1st of the month	*yihao (ee-how)*	一号
2nd of the month	*erri (urr-rr)*	二日
2nd of the month	*erhao (urr-how)*	二号
3rd of the month	*sanri (sahn-rr)*	三日
4th of the month	*siri (suh-rr)*	四日
5th of the month	*wuri (woo-rr)*	五日
6th of the month	*liuri (leo-rr)*	六日
7th of the month	*qiri (chee-rr)*	七日
8th of the month	*bari (bah-rr)*	八日
9th of the month	*jiuri (jeo-rr)*	九日
10th of the month	*shiri (shr-rr)*	十日
11th of the month	*shiyiri (shr-ee-rr)*	十一日
12th of the month	*shierri (shr-urr-rr)*	十二日
13th of the month	*shisanri (shr-sahn-rr)*	十三日
14th of the month	*shisiri (shr-suh-rr)*	十四日
15th of the month	*shiwuri (shr-woo-rr)*	十五日
16th of the month	*shiliuri (shr-leo-rr)*	十六日
17th of the month	*shiqiri (shr-chee-rr)*	十七日
18th of the month	*shibari (shr-bah-rr)*	十八日
19th of the month	*shijiuri (shr-jeo-rr)*	十九日

20th of the month	*ershiri (urr-shr-rr)*	二十日
21st of the month	*ershiyiri (urr-shr-ee-rr)*	二十一日
22nd of the month	*ershierri (urr-shr-urr-rr)*	二十二日
23rd of the month	*ershisanri (urr-shr-sahn-rr)*	二十三日
24th of the month	*ershisiri (urr-shr-suh-rr)*	二十四日
25th of the month	*ershiwuri (urr-shr-woo-rr)*	二十五日
26th of the month	*ershiliuri (urr-shr-leo-rr)*	二十六日
27th of the month	*ershiqiri (urr-shr-chee-rr)*	二十七日
28th of the month	*ershigari (urr-shr-bah-rr)*	二十八日
29th of the month	*ershijiuri (urr-shr-jeo-rr)*	二十九日
30th of the month	*sanshiri (sahn-shr-rr)*	三十日
31st of the month	*sanshiyiri (sahn-shr-ee-rr)*	三十一日

Today is the 7th.
Jintian shi qiri. 今天是七日。
(Jeen-tee-an shr chee-rr)

Holidays

New Year's Day   *Xin Nian (Sheen Nee-an)* 新年

Spring Festival (late January or early February)
Chun Jie 春节
(Choon Jee-eh)

International Women's Day, March 8
Guoji Funu Jie 国际妇女节
(Gwoh-jee Foo-nwee Jee-eh)

International Labor Day, May 1
Guoji Laodong Jie 国际劳动节
(Gwoh-jee Lao-dohng Jee-eh)

Youth Day, May 4
Qingnin Jie 青年节
(Cheeng-nee-an Jee-eh)

International Children's Day
Guoji Ertong Jie 国际儿童节
(Gwoh-jee Urr-tohng Jee-eh)

National Day, October 1
Guoqing Jie 国庆节
(Gwoh-cheeng Jee-eh)

PART 3

Countries

China   Zhongguo (Johng-gwoh) 中国
Chinese Language   Hanyu or Zhongwen* (Hahn-yuu /
                     Johng-wern) 汉语 / 中文

Hanyu is the literary term for the Chinese language; *Zhongwen* is
the term generally used in ordinary speech.

Chinese Person   Zhongguoren (Johng-gwoh-wren)
                     中国人
Overseas Chinese   Hua Qiao (Hwah Chee-ow) 华侨
Hong Kong   Xiang Gang (She-ahng Gahng) 香港
Kowloon   Jiulong (Jeo-lohng) 九龙
Macao   Aomen (Ow-mern) 澳门

Australia   Aodaliya (Ow-dah-lee-ah) 澳大利亚
Canada   Jianada (Jee-ah-nah-dah) 加拿大
France   Faguo (Fah-gwoh) 法国
Germany   Deguo (Der-gwoh) 德国
Great Britain   Yingguo (Eeng-gwoh) 英国
India   Yindu (Een-doo) 印度
Italy   Yidali (Ee-dah-lee) 意大利
Japan   Riben (Rr-burn) 日本
Spain   Xibanya (She-bahn-yah) 西班牙
United States   Meiguo (May-gwoh) 美国

China's Provinces

Anhui *(Ahn-hway)* 安徽
Fujian *(Foo-jee-ahn)* 福建
Gansu *(Gahn-soo)* 甘肃
Guangdong *(Gwahng-dohng)* 广东
Guizhou *(Gway-joe)* 贵州
Hainan *(High-nahn)* 海南
Hebei *(Her-bay)* 河北
Heilongjiang *(Hay-loong-jee-ahng)* 黑龙江
Henan *(Her-nahn)* 河南
Jiangxi *(Jee-ahng-she)* 江西
Jilin *(Jee-leen)* 吉林
Liaoning *(Lee-ow-neeng)* 辽宁
Qinghai *(Cheeng-high)* 青海
Shaanxi *(Shah-ahn-she)* 陕西
Shandong *(Shahn-dohng)* 山东
Shanxi *(Shah-she)* 山西
Sichuan *(Suh-chwahn)* 四川
Yunnan *(Ywun-nahn)* 云南
Zhejiang *(Juh-jee-ahng)* 浙江

The Autonomous Regions

Guangxi Zhuang *(Gwahng-she Jwahng)* 广西庄
Nei Menggu *(Nay Merng-goo)* 内蒙古
   (Inner Mongolia)
Ningxia *(Neeng-shee-ah)* 宁夏
Xizang *(Tibet)* *(She-zahng)* 西藏
Xinjiang *(Sheen-jee-ahng)* 新疆

Major Cities

Aomen / Macao *(Ow-mern)* 澳门
Beijing *(Bay-jeeng)* 北京
Changchun *(Chahng-choon)* 长春
Chungking / Chongqing *(Chohng-cheeng)* 重庆
Canton / Guangzhou *(Gwahng-joe)* 广州
Dalian *(Dah-lee-an)* 大连
Harbin *(Hah-urr-bin)* 哈尔滨
Hong Kong / Xiang Gang *(Shee-ahng Gahng)* 香港
Kunming *(Koon-meeng)* 昆明
Mukden / Shenyang *(Shern-Yahng)* 沈阳
Nanking / Nanjing *(Nahn-jeeng)* 南京
Shanghai *(Shahng-high)* 上海
Shenzhen *(Shern-jern)* 深圳
Tianjin *(Tee-an-jeen)* 天津
Urumqi *(Woo-roo-moo-chee)* 乌鲁木齐
Wuhan *(Woo-hahn)* 武汉
Xiamen / Amoy *(She-ah-mern)* 厦门

Famous Places in Beijing

Beijing Zoo
Beijing Dongwuyuan 北京动物园
(Bay-jeeng Dohng-woo-ywahn)

Forbidden City
Zijin Cheng 紫禁城
(Dzu-jeen Cherng)

Gate of Supreme Harmony
Tai He Men 太和门
(Tie Her Mern)

Great Hall of the People
Renmin Dahuitang 人民大会堂
(Wren-meen Dah-hway-tahng)

Imperial Gardens
Yuhua Yuan 御花园
(Yuu-hwah Ywahn)

Mao Zedong Memorial Mausoleum
Mao Zedong Jinian Tang 毛泽东纪念堂
(Mao Zuh-dohng Jee-nee-an Tahng)

Marco Polo Bridge
Lugou Qiao 路沟桥
(Loo-gwoh Chee-ow)

Museum of Chinese History
Zhongguo Lishi Bowuguan 中国历史博物馆
(Johng-gwoh Lee-shr Bwo-woo-gwahn)

National Library
Zhongguo Tushuguan 中国图书馆
(Johng-gwoh Too-shoo-gwahn)

Nationalities Cultural Palace
Minzu Wenhua Gong 民族文化宫
(Meen-joo Wern-hwah Gohng)

People's Cultural Park
Renmin Wenhua Gongyuan 人民文化公园
(Wren-meen Wern-hwah Gohng-ywahn)

Summer Palace
Yihe Yuan 颐和园
(Ee-her Ywahn)

Tiananmen Square
Tian An Men Guangchang 天安门广场
(Tee-an Ahn Mern Gwahng-chahng)

Xidan Market
Xidan Shichang 西淡市场
(She-dahn Shr-chahng)

Zhongshan Park
Zhongshan Gongyuan 中山公园
(Johng-shahn Gohng-ywahn)

Famous Landmarks Near Beijing

Great Wall of China
Chang Cheng　长城
(Chahng Churng)

Ming Tombs
Shi San Ling　十三陵
(Shr Sahn Leeng)

Shopping Districts in Beijing

Jianguomenwai
Jian Guo Men Wai　蒋国门外
(Jee-an Gwoh Mern Wigh)

Liulichang
Liu Li Chang　琉璃场
(Lee-oh Lee Chahng)

Qianmen
Qian Men　前门
(Chee-an Mern)

Wangfujing
Wang Fu Jing　王府井
(Wahng Foo Jeeng)

Xidan
Xi Dan　西淡
(She Dahn)

Famous Places in Shanghai

The Bund
Waitan Zhongshan Road   外滩中山路
(Wigh-tahn Johng-shahn Loo)

Fuxing Park
Fuxing Gongyuan   福星公园
(Foo-sheeng Gohng-ywahn)

Jade Buddha Temple
Yu Fo Si   玉佛寺
(Yuu fwo Suh)

Longhua Temple & Pagoda
Longhua Miao He Ta   龙华庙合塔
(Lohng-hwah Mee-ow Her Tah)

Lu Xun Memorial Museum
Lu Xun Jinian Guan   鲁迅纪念馆
(Loo Sheen Jee-nee-an Gwahn)

Old Town
Shanghai Jiu Shi   上海旧市
(Shahng-high Jeo Shr)

People's Park & Square
Renmin Guangchang   人民广场
(Wren-meen Gwahng-chahng)

Shanghai Acrobatic Theater
Shanghai Zajiyan Juyuan 上海杂技演剧院
(Shahng-high Zah-jee-yahn Jwee-ywahn)

Shanghai Children's Palace
Shanghai Shaonian Gong 上海少年宫
(Shahng-high Shou-nee-an Gohng)

Shanghai Exhibition Center
Shanghai Janlan Guan 上海展览馆
(Shahng-high Jahn-lahn Gwahn)

Shanghai Museum of Art & History
Shanghai Bowuguan-de Yishu he Lishi
(Shahng-high Bwo-woo-gwahn-duh ee-shoo her Lee-shr)
上海博物馆的艺术和历史

Sun Yat-sen Residence
Sun Zhongshan Guju 孙中山故居
(Soon Johng-shahn Goo-jwee)

Tomb of Soong Qingling
Song Qing-ling Fenmu 宋庆龄坟墓
(Soong Cheeng-leeng Fern-moo)

Worker's Cultural Palace
Gongren Wenhua Gong 工人文化宫
(Goong-wren Wun-hwah Goong)

Xijiao Park
Xi Jiao Gongyuan 西角园
(Shee Jee-ow Gohng-ywahn)

Yu Garden
Yu Yuan 玉园
(Yuu Ywahn)

Shopping Districts in Shanghai

Huaihai Road   *(Hwie-high Loo)* 淮海路
Nanjing Road   *(Nahn-jeeng Loo)* 南京路

Important Signs

Public signs are a phenomenon of the modern age. Without them, sophisticated societies simply wouldn't function, and it is especially important to be able to read and understand signs when visiting foreign countries. The following are provided to help visitors to China avoid being "sign illiterate."

Arrivals   *Jinguan (Jeen-gwahn)* 进关
Departures   *Chuguan (Choo-gwahn)* 出关
Customs   *Haiguan (High-gwahn)* 海关
Bathroom   *Yushi (Yuu-shr)* 浴室
Engaged (in use)   *Shiyongzhong (Shr-yohng-johng)*
                       使用中

Alley (narrow street)   *Hutong (Hoo-tohng)* 胡同
Bicycle Parking   *Cunche Chu (Tsoon-cher Choo)* 存车处
Bicycle Parking Zone   *Zixingche Cunchechu (Dzu-sheeng-cher Tsoon-cher-choo)* 自行车存车处

Car Parking Lot	*Tingche Chang (Teeng-cher Chahng)* 停车场
Closed Door	*Guan Men (Gwahn Mern)* 关门
Business Hours	*Yingye Shijian (Eeng-yeh Shr-jee-an)* 营业时间
Bus Stop	*Qiche Zhan (Chee-cher Jahn)* 汽车站
Caution	*Xiaoxin (She-ow-sheen)* 小心
Closed (business)	*Tingzhiyingye (Teeng-jr-eeng-yeh)* 停止营业
	Guanmen (Gwahn-mern) 关门
Danger	*Weixian (Way-shee-an)* 危险
Emergency Exit	*Jinji Chukou (Jeen-jee Choo-koe)* 紧急出口
	Taiping Men (Tie-peeng mern) 太平门
Entrance	*Rukou (Roo-koe)* 入口
Exit	*Chukou (Choo-koe)* 出口
Do Not Enter	*Buxu Jinru (Boo-shoo Jeen-roo)* 不许进入
Don't Touch	*Wuchu (Woo-choo)* 勿触
	Wumo (Woo-mwo) 勿抹
Drinking Water	*Yingyong Shui (Eeng-yohng Shway)* 饮用水
Elevator	*Dianti (Dee-an-tee)* 电梯
Employees Only	*Xianren Mianru (Shee-an-wren Mee-an-roo)* 闲人免入
First Aid	*Ji Jiu (Jee Jeo)* 急救
Forbidden	*Jinzhi (Jeen-jr)* 禁止
Hospital	*Yiyuan (Ee-ywahn)* 医院
Information	*Tongzhi (Tohng-jr)* 通知
Information Desk	*Xunwen tai (Shwun-wern tai)* 询问台
Information Office	*Xunwen chu (Shwun wun choo)* 讯问处

Keep Out	*Qie-wu Runei (Chee-eh woo Roo-nay)* 切勿入内
Ladies' Room	*Nu Cesuo (Nwee Tser-swoh)* 女厕所
Left Luggage Storage	*Xingli Jicun Chu (Sheeng-lee Jee-tsoon Choo)* 行李寄存处
Luggage Lockers	*Xingli Gui (Sheeng-lee Gway)* 行李柜
Main Street	*Dajie (Dah-jee-eh)* 大街
Men's Room	*Nan Cesuo (Nahn Tser-swoh)* 男厕所
Non-potable Water	*Fei Yingyong Shui (Fay Eeng-yohng Shway)* 非饮用水
No Entrance	*Jinzhi Runei (Jeen-jr Roo-nay)* 禁止入内
No Parking	*Bu Xutingche (Boo Shee-teeng-cher)* 不许停车
No Picture Taking	*Qing Wu Pai-zhao (Cheeng Woo Pie-jow)* 请勿拍照
No Smoking, Please	*Qing Wu Xiyan (Cheeng Woo She-yahn)* 请勿抽烟
No Spitting, Please	*Qing Wu Tutan (Cheeng Woo Too-tahn)* 请勿吐痰
No Trespassing	*Buzhun Runei (Boo-joon Roo-nay)* 不准入内
Open (for business)	*Yingye (Eeng-yeh)* 营业
Open Door	*Kai Men (Kigh Mern)* 开门
Please Don't Touch	*Qing Wu Dongshou (Cheeng Woo Dohng-show)* 请勿动手
Please Line Up	*Qing Paidui (Jeeng Pie-dway)* 请排队
Police	*Jingcha (Jeeng-chah)* 警察
Public Bath	*Gongyong Yu Chi (Gohng-yohng Yuu Chr)* 公用浴池
Public Telephone	*Gongyong dianhua (Gohng-yohng Dee-an-hwah)* 公用电话
Public Toilet	*Gongyong Cesuo (Gohng-yohng Tser-swoh)* 公用厕所

Pull (to open door)	*La (Lah)* 拉
Push (to open door)	*Tui (Tway)* 推
Reserved	*Yuyue (Yuu-yuu-eh)* 预约
Self-Service	*Zi-Zhu (Dzu-Joo)* 自助
Smoking Permitted	*Keyi Xiyan (Ker-ee She-yahn)* 可以吸烟
Sold Out	*Quan Man (Chwahn Mahn)* 全满
Full House	*Ke Man (Kuh Mahn)* 客满
Ticket Office	*Shoupiao Chu (Show-pee-ow Choo)* 售票处
Toilet	*Cesuo (Tser-swoh)* 厕所
Vacancy	*You Kong Fang (You Kohng Fahng)* 有空房
Waiting Room	*Xiuxi Shi (Sheo-she Shr)* 休息室
Welcome	*Huanying Guanglin (Hwahn-eeng Gwahng-leen)* 欢迎光临
Admission Free	*Mianfei Ruchang (Mee-an-fay Roo-chahng)* 免费入场

PART 4

Making Your Own Sentences

I want to go to _____ .
Wo yao qu _____ .　我要去 _____ 。
(I want to go to _____)

Please take me to _____ .
Qing dai wo dao _____ .　请带我到 _____ 。
(Cheeng die woh dow____)

Please pick me up at _____ .
Qing zai _____ *jie wo.*　请在 _____ 接我。
(Cheeng zigh _____ jee-eh woh)

Please come back at _____ .
Qing ____ *hui lai.*　请 ____ 回来。
(Cheeng ____ hwee lie)

Please give me _____ .
Qing gei wo _____ .　请给我 _____ 。
(Cheeng gay woh _____)

Please show me _____ .
Qing gei wo kan _____ .　请给我看 _____ 。
(Cheeng gay woh kahn _____)

I want to buy _____ .
Wo yao mai _____ .　我要买 _____ 。
(Woh yee-ow my _____)

Please bring me _____ .
Qing song _____ *lai.* 请送 _____ 来。
(Cheeng soong _____ lie)

I would like _____ .
Wo xiang yao _____ . 我想要 _____ 。
(Woh she-ahng yee-ow _____)

I am looking for _____ .
Wo zai zhao _____ . 我在找 _____ 。
(Woh zigh jow _____)

PART 5

Additional Vocabulary

[A]

abacus	*suanpan (swah-pahn)* 算盘	
abroad	*guowai (gwoh-wigh)* 国外	
accident	*shigu (she-goo)* 事故	
acupuncture	*zhenjiu (jern-jeo)* 针灸	
adaptor plug	*zhuanjie chatou (jwahn-jee-eh chatoe)* 转接插头	
address	*dizhi (dee-jr)* 地址	
address book	*tongxun bu (tohng-sheen boo)* 通讯部	
admission	*ruchang (roo-chahng)* 入场	
adult	*daren (dah-wren)* 大人	
age	*nianling (nee-an-leeng)* 年龄	
AIDS	*aizi bing (eye-dzu beeng)* 爱滋病	
air conditioner	*kongtiaoji (kohng-tee-ow-jee)* 空调机	
airline hostess	*hangkong gongsi (hahng-kohng gohng-suh)* 航空公司	
air pollution	*kongqi wuran (kohng-chee woo-rahn)* 空气污染	
airsick	*yunji (yuun-jee)* 晕机	
alarm clock	*nao zhong (nah-oh johng)* 闹钟	
alcohol	*jiu (jeo)* 酒	
allergic, allergy	*guomin (gwoh-meen)* 过敏	
alley (narrow street)	*hutong (hoo-tohng)* 胡同	
altitude	*haiba (high-bah)* 海拔	
ambassador	*dashi (dah-shr)* 大使	
ancient	*gudai (goo-die)* 古代	
anniversary	*zhounian jinian (joe-nee-an jee-nee-an)* 周年纪念	

announcement	*diantai huo (dee-an-tie hwah)* 电台话
antibiotic	*kangshengsu (kahng-sherng-soo)* 抗生素
antique store	*gudong dian (goo-dohng dee-an)* 古董店
apartment	*danyuan fang (dahn-ywahn fahng)* 单元房
appendicitis	*mangchang yan (mahng chahng yahn)* 盲肠炎
appetite	*shiyu (shr-yuu)* 食欲
appetizer	*lengpan (lerng-pahn)* 冷盘
application	*shengqing (sherng-cheeng)* 申请
application form	*shengqing biao (sherng-cheeng bee-ow)* 申请表
appointment	*yuehui (yu-eh hway)* 约会
area / district	*yidai (ee-die)* 一带
army	*jundui (jwin-dway)* 军队
arrive	*daoda (dow-dah)* 到达
art	*yishu (ee-shoo)* 艺术
art gallery	*hualang (hwah-lahng)* 画廊
artist	*yishujia (ee-shoo-jee-ah)* 艺术家
art museum	*meishu guan (may-shoo gwahn)* 美术馆
arts & crafts	*gongyi meishu (gohng-ee may-shoo)* 工艺美术
Asia	*Yazhou (Yah-joe)* 亚洲
aspirin	*asipilin (ah-suh-pee-leen)* 阿司匹林
asthma	*qichuanbing (chee-chwahn-beeng)* 气喘病
athletics	*yundong (ywun-dohng)* 运动
attorney	*lushi (lwee-shr)* 律师
audience	*guanzhong (gwahn-johng)* 观众
auditorium	*litang (lee-tahng)* 礼堂
authentic	*kekao (ker-kow)* 可靠
author	*zuozhe (zwoh-juh)* 作者

authorize	*shouchuan* (show-chwahn) 授权
automobile	*qiche* (chee-cher) 汽车
avenue	*dajie* (dah-jee-eh) 大街

[B]

baby	*yinger* (eeng-urr) 婴儿
baby food	*yinger shipin* (eeng-urr shr-peen) 婴儿食品
bachelor	*danshenhan* (dahn-shern-hahn) 单身汉
back door	*hou men* (hoe mern) 后门
bad quality	*cha* (chah) 差
bag	*daizi* (die-dzu) 袋子
baggage	*xingli* (sheeng-lee) 行李
baggage cart	*xingli che* (sheeng-lee cher) 行李车
baggage claim	*xingli ting* (sheeng-lee teeng) 行李厅
baggage tag	*xingli pai* (sheeng-lee pie) 行李牌
bakery	*mianbao dian* (mee-an-bow dee-an) 面包店
ball game	*qui sai* (cheo sigh) 球赛
ballroom	*wuting* (woo-teeng) 舞厅
bamboo shoots	*zhusun* (joo-soon) 竹笋
banana	*xiangiao* (shee-ahng-jee-ow) 香蕉
band (musical)	*yuedui* (yu-eh-dway) 乐队
bandage	*bengdai* (bung-die) 绷带
band-aid	*zhixue jiaobu* (jr-shu-eh jee-ow-boo) 止血胶布
bank	*yinhang* (een-hahng) 银行
banquet	*yanhui* (yahn-hway) 宴会
banquet room	*yanhui ting* (yahn-hway teeng) 宴会厅
bar (drinking)	*jiuba* (jeo-bah) 酒吧
barbecue	*kao* (kow) 烤
baseball	*hangqiu* (hahng-chee-oh) 棒球
basketball	*lanqui* (lahn-chee-oh) 篮球

bath	*yugang (yuu-gahng)*	浴缸
bathing suit	*youyongyi (you-yohng-ee)*	游泳衣
bathrobe	*yuyi (yuu-yee)*	浴衣
bathroom	*yushi (yuu-shr)*	浴室
bath towel	*xizao maojin (she-zow mao-jeen)* 洗澡毛巾	
bathtub	*zaopen (zow-pern)*	澡盆
bean curd	*doufu (doe-foo)*	豆腐
beef	*niurou (new-roe)*	牛肉
beefsteak	*niu pai (new pie)*	牛排
beer	*pijiu (pee-jeo)*	啤酒
bell captain	*xingli lingban (sheeng-lee leeng-bahn)* 行李领班	
bicycle	*zixingche (dzu-sheeng-cher)*	自行车
blister	*pao (pow)*	疱
blood pressure	*xueya (shu-eh-yah)*	血压
boarding pass	*dengji pai (derng-jee pie)*	登机牌
boat	*chuan (chwahn)*	船
boiled water	*kai shui (kigh shway)*	开水
book	*shu (shoo)*	书
bookkeeper	*kuaiji (kwie-jee)*	会计
bookshop	*shu dian (shoo dee-an)*	书店
border	*bianjie (bee-an-jay)*	边界
bottle	*ping (peeng)*	瓶
bottle opener	*kaipingqi (kigh-peeng-chee)*	开瓶器
boulevard	*dadao (dah-dow)*	大道
box	*hezi (her-dzu)*	盒子
boyfriend	*nanpengyou (nahn-perng-you)*	男朋友
branch office	*fen gongsi (fern gohng-suh)*	分公司
brand, trademark	*shangbiao (shahng-bee-ow)*	商标
bride	*xinniang (sheen-nee-ahng)*	新娘
brother	*xiongdi (she-ong-dee)*	兄弟
Buddhism	*Fojiao (Fwo-jee-ow)*	佛教

budget	*yusuan (yuu-swahn)* 预算
Buddhist	*Fojiao (Fwo-jee-ow)* 佛教
buffet	*zizhucan (dzu-joo-tsahn)* 自助餐
buffet lunch / dinner	*zizhu wucan (dzu-joo woo-tsahn)* 自助午餐
building	*loufang (low-fahng)* 楼房
business	*shangye (shahng-yeh)* 商业
business person	*shang ren (shahng wren)* 商人

[C]

cable television	*bilu dianshi (bee-loo dee-an-shr)* 秘露电视
café	*kafeiguan (kah-fay-gwahn)* 咖啡馆
cafeteria	*shitang (shr-tahng)* 食堂
calendar	*rili (rr-lee)* 日历
lunar calendar	*yinli (een-lee)* 阴历
California	*Jiazhou (Jee-ah-joe)* 加洲
calligraphy	*shufa (shoo-fah)* 书法
calculator	*jisuanji (jee-swahn-jee)* 计算机
camera	*zhaoxiangji (jow-shee-ahng-jee)* 照相机
canal	*yunhe (yuun-her)* 运河
cancer	*aizheng (eye-jerng)* 癌症
captain (plane)	*jizhang (jee-jahng)* 机长
captain (ship)	*chuanzhang (chwahn-jahng)* 船长
cash (money)	*xianjin (shee-an-jeen)* 现金
cashier	*caiwu (tsigh-woo)* 财务
casual	*suibian (sway-bee-an)* 随便
cattle	*shengkou (sherng-koe)* 牲口
centigrade	*sheshi (sher-shr)* 摄氏
central heating	*jizhong gongre (jee-johng gohng-rr)* 集中供热
cereal	*maipian (my-pee-an)* 麦片

ceremony	*dianli (dee-in-lee)*	典礼
chair	*yizi (eed-dzu)*	椅子
change (money)	*lingqian (leeng-chee-in)*	零钱
changing money	*duihuan (dway-hwahn)*	兑换
check (noun)	*zhipiao (jr-pee-ow)*	支票
check	*jiancha (jee-an cha)*	检察
cheongsam (dress)	*qipao (chee-pow)*	旗袍
children	*haizimen (high-dzu-mern)*	孩子们
Chinese characters / ideograms	*hanzi (hahn-jee)*	汉字
Chinese language	*Han you (Hahn yuu)*	汉语
Chinese (people)	*Zhonguoren (Johng-gwoh wren)*	中国人
chocolate	*qiaokeli (chee-ow-ker-lee)*	巧克力
chopsticks	*kuaizi (kwie-dzu)*	筷子
church	*jiaotang (jee-ow-tahng)*	教堂
city, town	*chengshi (churng-shr)*	城市
city tour	*youlan shirong (you-lahn shr-roong)*	游览市容
class (students)	*ban (bahn)*	班
classmate	*tongxue (tohng-shu-eh)*	同学
cloakroom	*yimaojian (ee-mao-jee-an)*	衣帽间
clock	*zhong (johng)*	钟
closing time	*guan men (gwahn mern)*	关门
coach, bus	*changtuqiche (chahng-too-chee-cher)*	长途汽车
coal	*mei (may-ee)*	煤
coastline	*haian xian (high-ahn shee-an)*	海岸线
coat	*dayi (dah-ee)*	大衣
cocktail	*jiweijiu (jee-way-jeo)*	鸡尾酒
cocktail party	*jiweijiuhui (jee-way-jeo-hway)*	鸡尾酒会
college, university	*dazue (dah-shu-eh)*	大学
compartment	*chexiang (cher-shee-ahng)*	车厢

company, firm	*gongsi (gohng-suh)*	公司
competition	*jingzheng (jeeng-jerng)*	竞争
computer	*diannao (dee-an-now)*	电脑
concert	*yinyuehui (een-yuu-eh-hway)*	音乐会
conductor (bus)	*shoupiaoyuan (show-pee-ow-ywahn)*	
	售票员	
conference	*huiyi (hway-ee)*	会议
conference room	*huiyi shi (hway-ee shr)*	会议室
Confucius	*Kongzi (Kohng-dzu)*	孔子
congratulations	*gongxi (gohng-she)*	恭喜
consulate	*lingshiguan (leeng-shr-gwahn)*	领事馆
contract	*hetong (her-tohng)*	合同
conversation	*huihua (hwee-hwah)*	会话
corner (street)	*guaijiao (gwie-jee-ow)*	拐角
cough drops	*kesou tang (ker-soe tahng)*	咳嗽糖
counter (sales)	*guitai (gway-tie)*	柜台
country (nation)	*guojia (gwoh-jee-ah)*	国家
couple (married)	*fufu (foo-foo)*	夫妇
credit card	*xinyong ka (sheen-yohng kah)*	信用卡
crowd	*renqun (wren-chwun)*	人群
crowded	*yongji (yohng-jee)*	拥挤
cultural exchange	*wenhua jiaoliu (wern-hwah jee-ow-leo)*	
	文化交流	
culture	*wenhua (wern-hwah)*	文化
cultural relic	*wenhua guji (wern-hwah goo-jee)*	
	文化古迹	
custom, ways	*fengsu (ferng-soo)*	风俗
Customs	*Haiguan (High-gwahn)*	海关
Customs tariff	*Guanshui shuize (Gwahn-shway shway-zuh)*	
	关税税则	

[D]

daily paper	*ri bao (rr bow)*	日报

dance hall	*wu ting (woo teeng)*	舞厅
dance party	*wu hui (woo hway)*	舞会
dangerous	*weixian (way-shee-an)*	危险
date /meeting	*yuehui (yu-eh-hway)*	约会
courting	*tan lian ai (tahn-lee-an aye)*	谈恋爱
daytime	*baitian (buy-tee-an)*	白天
degree (college)	*xuewei (shu-eh-way)*	学位
delicatessen	*shushi dian (shoo-shr dee-an)*	熟食店
demonstration	*shiwei (shr-way)*	示威
dentist	*yayi (yah-ee)*	牙医
department (company)	*bu (boo)*	部
department store	*baihuo dian (by-hwoh dee-an)*	百货店
departure	*chufa (choo-fah)*	出发
deposit (money)	*yajin (yah-jeen)*	押金
desk	*shuzhuo (shoo-jwoh)*	书桌
dessert	*tianpin (tee-an-peen)*	甜品
diarrhoea	*fuxie (foo-she-eh)*	腹泻
dictionary	*zidian (dzu-dee-an)*	字典
dining car	*canche (tsahn-cher)*	餐车
dining room	*can ting (tsahn teeng)*	餐厅
diplomat	*waijiaojia (wigh-jee-ow-jee-ah)*	外交家
discount	*zhekou (juh-koe)*	折扣
domestic	*guonei (gwoh-nay)*	国内
door, gate	*men (mern)*	门
Dragon Boat Festival	*Duan Wu Jie (Dwahn Woo Jee-eh)*	端午节
drink (noun)	*yinliao (een-lee-ow)*	饮料
drinking straw	*xiguanr (she-gwahn-urr)*	吸管
driver	*siji (suh-jee)*	司机
driver's license	*jiashi zhizhao (jee-ah-shr jr-jow)*	驾驶执照
drugstore	*yaodian (yee-ow-dee-an)*	药店
drunk	*zui (zway)*	醉

dry clean	*gan xi (gahn she)* 干洗
dry cleaner's	*gan xi dian (gahn she dee-an)* 干洗店
dust	*huichen (hway-churn)* 灰尘
dusty	*huichenduo (hway-churn-dwoh)* 灰尘多

[E]

ear ache	*erduo tong (urr-dwoh tohng)* 耳朵痛
earthquake	*dizhen (dee-jern)* 地震
East China Sea	*Dong Hai (Dohng High)* 东海
economy	*jingji (jeeng-jee)* 经济
editor	*bianji (bee-an-jee)* 编辑
education	*jiaoyu (jee-ow-yuu)* 教育
eel	*manyu (mahn-yuu)* 鳗鱼
egg	*jidan (jee-dahn)* 鸡蛋
election	*xuanju (shwen-jwee)* 选举
electric fan	*dian fengshan (dee-an ferng-shahn)* 电风扇
electric heater	*dian reqi (dee-an rr-chee)* 电热器
elevator	*dianti (dee-an-tee)* 电梯
embassy	*dashiguan (dah-shr-gwahn)* 大使馆
emergency	*jinjishijian (jeen-jee-shr-jee-an)* 紧急事件
emergency door	*taiping men (tie-peeng mern)* 太平门
emergency room	*jizhen shi (jee-jern shr)* 急诊室
employee	*gongzuorenyuan (gohng-zwoh-wren-ywahn)* 工作人员
energy	*nengliang (nerng-lee-ahng)* 能量
England	*Yingguo (Eeng-gwoh)* 英国
English language	*Yingwen (Eeng-wern)* 英文
entertain (guests)	*daike (die-ker)* 待客
envelope	*xinfeng (sheen-ferng)* 信封
environment	*huanjing (hwahn-jeeng)* 环境
Europe	*Ouzhou (Oh-joe)* 欧洲

European	*Ouzhouren (Oh-joe-wren)* 欧洲人
exchange rate	*duihuan lu (dway-hwahn lwee)* 兑换率
exhausted	*leihuai-le (lay-hwie-ler)* 累坏了
Exhibition Hall	*Zhanlan guan (Jahn-lahn gwahn)* 展览馆
exit	*chukou (choo-koe)* 出口
expenses	*feiyong (fay-yohng)* 费用
expensive	*gui (gway)* 贵
expert	*shulian (shoo-lee-an)* 熟练
export	*chukou (choo-koe)* 出口
extension cord	*jiechang dianxian (jee-eh-chahng dee-an-she-an)* 结长电线
extension phone	*fenji (fern-jee)* 分机
eyedrops	*yanyaoshui (yahn-yee-ow-shway)* 眼药水
eyeglasses	*yanjing (yahn-jeeng)* 眼镜

[F]

face	*lian (lee-an)* 脸
factory	*gongchang (gohng-chahng)* 工厂
Fahrenheit	*Huashi (Hwah-shr)* 华氏
fail	*shibai (Shr-by)* 失败
fake	*maopai (mao-pie)* 冒牌
false	*jiade (jee-ah-der)* 假的
family members	*qin ren (cheen wren)* 亲人
famous dish	*ming cai (meeng tsigh)* 名菜
far	*yuan (ywahn)* 远
farmer	*nongfu (nohng-foo)* 农夫
fast food	*kuai can (kwie tsahn)* 快餐
fashion	*shimao (shr-mao)* 时髦
father	*fuqin (foo-cheen)* 父亲
fault	*cuo (tswoh)* 错
fee, expense	*feiyong (fay-yohng)* 费用

female	*nu (nwee)* 女	
ferry	*duchuan (doo-chwahn)* 渡船	
festival	*jieri (jee-eh-rr)* 节日	
fever	*fashao (fah-shou)* 发烧	
fiancé	*weihunfu (way-hoon-foo)* 未婚夫	
fiancée	*weihunqi (way-hoon-chee)* 未婚妻	
film (camera)	*jiaojuan (jee-ow-jwahn)* 胶卷	
film (movie)	*dianying (dee-an-eeng)* 电影	
fine, penalty	*fakuan (fah-kwahn)* 罚款	
fire	*houzai (hwoh-zigh)* 火灾	
firecracker	*bianpao (bee-an-pow)* 鞭炮	
fire alarm	*huo jing (hwoh jeeng)* 火警	
fire escape	*anquan ti (ahn-chwahn tee)* 安全梯	
fire exit	*taiping men (tie-peeng mern)* 太平门	
first-aid kit	*ji jiu xiang (jee jeo shee-ahng)* 急救箱	
fish	*yu (yuu)* 鱼	
fisherman	*yumin (yuu-meen)* 渔民	
fishing boat	*yu chuan (yuu chwahn)* 渔船	
flag	*qizi (chee-dzu)* 旗子	
flood	*shuizai (shway-zigh)* 水灾	
flu	*ganmao (gahn-mao)* 感冒	
fly (insect)	*cangying (tsahng-eeng)* 苍蝇	
folk dance	*minjian wudao (meen-jee-an woo-dow)* 民间舞蹈	
food	*shiwu (shr-woo)* 食物	
food poisoning	*shiwu zhongdu (shr-woo joong-doo)* 食物中毒	
football (American)	*ganlanqiu (gahn-lahn-cheo)* 橄榄球	
football (soccer)	*zuqiu (joo-cheo)* 足球	
forecast	*yubao (yuu-bow)* 预报	
foreign exchange	*waihui (wigh-hway)* 外汇	
forest	*shulin (shoo-leen)* 树林	
form (printed)	*biaoge (bee-ow-guh)* 表格	

France	*Faguo (Fah-gwoh)*	法国
free (cost)	*mianfei (mee-ann-fay)*	免费
free trade zone	*ziyou maoyiqu (dzu-you mao-ee-chwee)*	
	自由贸易区	
freezing	*bingdong (beeng-dohng)*	冰冻
fresh	*xinxian (sheen-shee-an)*	新鲜
frozen food	*lengcang shipin (lerng-tsahng shr-peen)*	
	冷藏食品	
fruit	*shuiguo (shway-gwoh)*	水果
fruit juice	*guozhi (gwoh-jr)*	果汁
[G]		
gallon	*jialun (jee-ah-loon)*	加仑
game, match	*qiusai (cheo-sigh)*	球赛
garlic	*suan (swahn)*	蒜
gasoline	*qiyou (chee-you)*	汽油
gas station	*jiayou zhan (jee-ah-you jahn)*	加油站
genuine	*zhende (jern-der)*	真的
German	*Dewen (Der-wern)*	德文
Germany	*Deguo (Der-gwoh)*	德国
gift	*liwu (lee-woo)*	礼物
ginger	*jiang (jee-ahng)*	姜
ginseng	*renshen (wren-shern)*	人参
girlfriend	*nupengyou (nwee-perng-you)*	女朋友
glasses (eye)	*yanjing (yahn-jeeng)*	眼镜
gloves	*shoutao (show-tao)*	手套
golf	*gaoerfuqiu (gow-urr-foo-cheo)*	高尔夫球
government	*zhengfu (jerng-foo)*	政府
government office	*jiguan (jee-gwahn)*	机官
Grand Canal	*Da Yunhe (Dah Ywun-her)*	大运河
grandfather	*zufu (zoo-foo)*	祖父
grandmother	*zumu (zoo-moo)*	祖母
grandparents	*zufumu (zoo-foo-moo)*	祖父母

Great Wall	*Chang Cheng (Chahng Churng)*	长城
green tea	*lu cha (lwee chah)*	绿茶
group	*tuanti (twahn-tee)*	团体
guarantee	*baozheng (bow-jerng)*	保证
guest	*keren (ker-wren)*	客人
guest house	*binguan (bin-gwahn)*	宾馆
guide	*daoyou (dow-you)*	导游
guidebook	*luyou zhinan (luu-yoe jr-nahn)* 旅游指南	
gymnasium	*tiyuguan (tee-yuu-gwahn)*	体育馆

[H]
hall, meeting	*guan (gwahn)*	馆
handbag	*shoutibao (show-tee-bow)*	手提包
handicraft	*shougongyi pin (show-gohng-ee peen)* 手工艺品	
Happy Birthday	*shengri kuaile (sherng-rr-kwie-ler)* 生日快乐	
harbor	*gangwan (gahng-wahn)*	港湾
harvest	*shoucheng (show-churng)*	收成
hay fever	*huafen re (hwah-fern rr)*	花粉热
health club	*jianshen fang (jee-an-shern fahng)* 健身房	
heart attack	*xinzangbing fazuo (sheen-zahng-beeng fah-zwoh)* 心脏病发作	
heater	*nuanqi (nwahn-chee)*	暖气
heavy	*zhong (johng)*	重
highschool	*zhong xue (johng shu-eh)*	中学
highway	*gonglu (gohng-loo)*	公路
hire, rent	*zu (joo)*	租
hitchhike	*dache (dah-cher)*	搭车
hobby	*aihao (aye-how)*	爱好
holiday	*jiaqi (jee-ah-chee)*	假期

home	*jia (jee-ah, jah)* 家	
hometown	*guxiang (goo-shee-ahng)* 故乡	
honey	*fengmi (ferng-me)* 蜂蜜	
Hong Kong	*Xiang Gang (Shee-ahng Gahng)* 香港	
hospital	*yiyuan (ee-ywahn)* 医院	
host, owner	*zhuren (joo-wren)* 主人	
hot towel	*re maojin (rr mao-jeen)* 热毛巾	
hot water	*re shui (rr shway)* 热水	
house	*fangwu (fahng-woo)* 房屋	
hungry	*e (uh)* 饿	
hurry	*henji (hern-jee)* 很急	
hurt, ache	*teng (terng)* 疼	

[I]

ice	*bing (beeng)* 冰
ice cream	*bing qilin (beeng chee-leen)* 冰淇淋
ice water	*bing shui (beeng shway)* 冰水
ill, sick	*youbing (you-beeng)* 有病
illegal	*buhefa (boo-her-fah)* 不和法
immediately	*mashang (mah-shahng)* 马上
Imperial Palace	*Gu Gong (Goo Goong)* 故宫
import (item)	*jinkou (jeen-koe)* 进口
important	*zhongyao (johng-yow)* 重要
impossible	*bukenneng (boo-ker-nerng)* 不可能
incorrect	*budui (boo-dway)* 不对
industry	*gongye (gohng-yeh)* 工业
infected	*ganran (gahn-rahn)* 感染
inflammation	*fayan (fah-yahn)* 发炎
informal	*feizhenshi (fay-jern-shr)* 非正式
information desk	*wenxun chu (wern-sheen choo)* 问讯处
injection	*zhushe (joo-sher)* 注射
injured	*shoushang-le (show-shahng-ler)* 受伤了
insect repellent	*chuchongji (choo-chohng-jee)* 除虫剂

insurance	*baoxian (bow-shee-an)* 保险
international	*guoji (gwoh-jee)* 国际
interpreter	*fanyi (fahn-ee)* 翻译
intersection	*shizilukou (shr-dzu-loo-koe)* 十字路口
invitation	*qingtie (cheeng-tee-eh)* 请帖

[J]

jacket	*duanshangyi (dwahn-shahng-ee)* 短上衣
jade	*yu (yuu)* 玉
jail, prison	*jianyu (jee-an-yuu)* 监狱
jeans	*niuzaiku (new-zigh-koo)* 牛仔裤
jewelry	*zhubao (joo-bow)* 珠宝
jogging suit	*yundongyi (ywun-dohng-ee)* 运动衣
journalist	*jizhe (jee-juh)* 记者
journey	*luxing (lwee-sheeng)* 旅行
judge (noun)	*faguan (fah-gwahn)* 法官
judo	*roudao (roe-dow)* 柔道
juice (fruit)	*guozhi (gwoh-jr)* 果汁
jumper, sweater	*maoyi (mao-ee)* 毛衣
jungle	*conglin (tsohng-leen)* 丛林
justice	*gongzheng (gohng-jerng)* 公正

[K]

karate	*kongshoudao (kohng-show-dow)* 空手道
key	*yaoshi (yee-ow-shr)* 钥匙
kilogram	*gongjin (gohng-jeen)* 公斤
kindergarten	*youeryuan (you-urr-ywahn)* 幼儿园
kitchen	*chufang (choo-fahng)* 厨房
kite	*fengzheng (ferng-jerng)* 风筝
kleenex	*Zhijin (jr-jeen)* 纸巾
knee	*xigai (she-guy)* 膝盖
knife	*daozi (dow-dzu)* 刀子

| Korea | *Chaoxian (Chow-she-an)* 朝鲜 |
| Kyoto | *Jingdu (Jeeng-doo)* 京都 |

[L]

label	*biaoqian (bee-ow-chee-an)* 标签
lacquerware	*qiqi (chee-chee)* 漆器
lake	*hu (hoo)* 湖
lamb (meat)	*yangrou (yahng-roe)* 羊肉
landlord	*fangzhu (fahng-joo)* 房主
lane	*hutong (hoo-tohng)* 胡同
language	*yuyan (yuu-yahn)* 语言
late	*wan (wahn)* 晚
Latin America	*Lading Meizhou (Lah-deeng May-joe)* 拉丁美洲
laundry (clothing)	*yaoxi-de yifu (yee-ow-she-der ee-foo)* 要洗的衣服
laundry (place)	*xiyi dian (she-ee dee-an)* 洗衣店
law	*falu (fah-lwee)* 法律
lawyer	*lushi (lwee-shr)* 律师
leather	*pige (pee-guh)* 皮革
leave a message	*liu hua (leo hwah)* 留话
lecture	*jiangyan (jee-ahng-yahn)* 讲演
leg	*tui (tway)* 腿
legal	*hefa (her-fah)* 合法
leisure time	*kongxian shijian (kohng-shee-an shr-jee-an)* 空闲时间
lemon	*ningmeng (neeng-merng)* 柠檬
lend	*jie (jee-eh)* 借
lens (camera)	*jingtou (jeeng-toe)* 镜头
lens cap	*jingtougai (jeeng-toe-guy)* 镜头盖
letter	*xin (sheen)* 信
letter paper	*xin zhi (sheen jr)* 信纸
library	*tushuguan (too-shoo-gwahn)* 图书馆

license	*zuke zheng (joo-tser-jerng)* 注册证
lipstick	*kouhong (koe-hohng)* 口红
liquor	*baijiu (by-jeo)* 白酒
liter	*sheng (sherng)* 升
living room	*ke ting (ker teeng)* 客厅
lock	*suo (swoh)* 锁
long-distance	*changtu (chahng-too)* 长途
longevity	*changshou (chahng-show)* 长寿
Los Angeles	*Luo Shanji (Lwoh Shan-jee)* 洛杉矶
lost	*shiwu (shr-woo)* 失物
lost and found	*shiwu zhaoling (shr-woo jow-leeng)* 失物招领
loud	*chao (chow)* 吵
lounge	*xiuxishi (shew-she-shr)* 休息室
love	*ai (aye)* 爱
luggage	*xingli (sheeng-lee)* 行李
luggage rack	*xingli jia (sheeng-lee jee-ah)* 行李夹
lunar calendar	*yin li (een lee)* 阴历
lunch	*zhongfan (hohng-fahn)* 中饭
lung	*fei (fay)* 肺

[M]

Macao	*Aomen (Ow-mern)* 澳门
magazine	*zazhi (zah-jr)* 杂志
mahjong	*majiang (mah-jee-ahng)* 麻将
mail (noun)	*youjian (you-jee-an)* 邮件
mainland	*dalu (dah-loo)* 大陆
main station	*zhongzhan (johng-jahng)* 终站
maitre'd	*zongguan (zohng-gwahn)* 总管
manager	*jingli (jeeng-lee)* 经理
management	*guanli (gwahn-lee)* 管理
man-made	*ren-zao (wren-zow)* 人造
manufacture	*shengchan (sherng-chahn)* 生产

map	*ditu (dee-too)* 地图
market	*shichang (shr-chahng)* 市场
married	*yijing jiehun-de (ee-jeeng jee-eh-hwun-duh)* 已经结婚的
martial arts	*wu shu (woo shoo)* 武术
mask (for mouth)	*kouzhao (kow-jow)* 口罩
massage	*anmo (ahn-mwo)* 按摩
meal	*fan (fahn)* 饭
mechanic	*jigong (jee-gohng)* 技工
medicine	*yiyao (ee-yee-ow)* 医药
meeting	*hui (hway)* 会
message	*liuhua (leo-hwah)* 留话
meter	*gongchi (gohng-chr)* 公尺
microphone	*huatong (hwah-tohng)* 话筒
military	*junshi (jwin-shr)* 军事
milk	*niunai (new-nigh)* 牛奶
mineral water	*kuangquan shui (kwahng-chwahn shway)* 矿泉水
miniskirt	*chao duanqun (chow dwahn-chwun)* 超短裙
minority (people)	*shaoshu minzu (shou-shoo meen-joo)* 少数民族
mirror	*jingzi (jeeng-dzu)* 镜子
mistake	*cuowu (tswoh-woo)* 错误
model (person)	*moter (mwo-ter-urr)* 模特儿
money	*qian (chee-an)* 钱
monk	*heshang (her-shahng)* 和尚
monkey	*houzi (hoe-dzu)* 猴子
monosodium glutamate	*weijing (way-jeeng)* 味精
monument	*jinianbei (jee-nee-an-bay)* 纪念碑
mosquitos	*wenzi (wern-dzu)* 蚊子
mountain	*shan (shahn)* 山

movie	*dianying (dee-an-eeng)* 电影
movie theater	*dianying yuan (dee-an-eeng ywahn)* 电影院
museum	*bowuguan (bwo-woo-gwahn)* 博物馆
music	*yinyue (een-yu-eh)* 音乐
Muslim	*Huijiaotu (Hway-jee-ow-too)* 回教徒
mutton	*yangrou (yahng-roe)* 羊肉

[N]

nail clippers	*zhijiadao (jr-jee-ah-dow)* 趾甲刀
name	*xingming (sheeng-meeng)* 姓名
nap	*xiaoshui (she-ow-shway)* 小睡
napkin	*canjin (tsahn-jeen)* 餐巾
nation	*guo (gwoh)* 国
national	*guojia (gwoh-jee-ah)* 国家
nationality	*minzu (meen-joo)* 民族
native dress	*guofu (gwoh-foo)* 国服
native place	*kuxiang (koo-she-ahng)* 故乡
navy	*haijun (high-jwin)* 海军
near	*jin (jeen)* 近
neck	*bozi (bwo-dzu)* 脖子
necklace	*xianglian (she-ahng-lee-an)* 项链
necktie	*lingdai (leeng-die)* 领带
neighbor	*linju (leen-jwee)* 邻居
newspaper	*baozhi (bow-jr)* 报纸
New Year's Eve	*Xin Nian Yuandan (Sheen Nee-an Ywahn-dahn)* 新年元旦
nightclub	*ye zonghui (yeh johng-hway)* 夜总会
nightlife	*ye shenghuo (yeh sherng-hwoh)* 夜生活
noodles	*miantiao (mee-an-tee-ow)* 面条
noodle shop	*mian guan (mee-an gwahn)* 面馆
noon	*zhongwu (johng-woo)* 中午
North America	*Bei Meizhou (Bay May-joe)* 北美洲

Northeast China	*Dong Bei (Dohng Bay)*	东北
notebook	*bijiben (bee-jee-burn)*	笔记本
novel (book)	*xiaoshuo (shee-ow-shwo)*	小说
novelist	*xiaoshuojia (shee-ow-shwo-jee-ah)* 小说家	
nurse	*hushi (hoo-shr)*	护士
nursery	*tuoersuo (twoh-urr-swoh)*	托儿所

[O]

oatmeal	*maipian (my-pee-an)*	麦片
ocean	*haiyang (high-yahng)*	海洋
office	*bangongshi (bahn-gohng-shr)*	办公室
office hours	*bangong shijian (bahn-gohng shr-jee-an)* 办公时间	
official business	*gong wu (gohng woo)*	公务
oil	*you (you)*	油
oil field	*you tian (yoe tee-an)*	油田
ointment	*yaogao (yee-ow-gow)*	药膏
one-way	*dan-cheng (dahn-churng)*	单程
one-way ticket	*dan-cheng piao (dahn-churng pee-ow)* 单程票	
open (shop)	*kaimen (kigh-mern)*	开门
opera	*geju (guh-jwee)*	歌剧
Beijing opera	*jingju (jeeng-jwee)*	京剧
orange juice	*juzi zhi (jwee-dzu jr)*	橘子汁
ordinary train	*putong che (poo-tohng cher)*	普通车
outlet (electric)	*chazuo (chah-zwoh)*	插座
out of order	*huaile (hwie-ler)*	坏了
outside line	*wai xian (wigh shee-an)*	外线
overcoat	*dayi (dah-ee)*	大衣
overnight	*guoye (gwoh-yeh)*	过夜
overseas	*guowai (gwoh-wigh)*	国外
Overseas Chinese	*Hua Qiao (Hwah Chee-ow)*	华侨

overseas edition	*haiwai ban* (high-wigh- bahn)	海外板
owner	*suoyouren* (swoh-you-wren)	所有人

[P]

Pacific Ocean	*Taiping Yang* (Tie-peeng Yahng) 太平洋	
package	*baoguo* (bow-gwoh)	包裹
pagoda	*baota* (bow-tah)	宝塔
painful	*henteng* (hern-terng)	很疼
panda bear	*xiong mao* (shee-ong mao)	熊猫
paper	*zhi* (jr)	纸
parents	*fumu* (foo-moo)	父母
Paris	*Bali* (Bah-lee)	巴黎
parking lot	*tingche chang* (teeng-cher chahng) 停车场	
partner	*huoban* (hwoh-bahn)	伙伴
party (gathering)	*jihui* (jwee-hway)	聚会
passenger	*luke* (lwee-ker)	旅客
passport	*huzhao* (hoo-jow)	护照
passport number	*huzhao haoma* (hoo-jow how-mah) 护照号码	
pastry	*gaodian* (gow-dee-an)	糕点
pastry shop	*gaodian dian* (gow-dee-an dee-an) 糕点店	
patient	*bingren* (beeng-wren)	病人
peanuts	*huasheng* (hwah-sherng)	花生
Pearl River	*Zhu Jiang* (Joo Jee-ahng)	珠江
Peking duck	*Beijing kaoya* (Bay-jeeng kow-yah) 北京烤鸭	
performer	*yanyuan* (yahn-ywahn)	演员
permission	*xuke* (shee-ker)	许可
permit (allow)	*yunxu* (ywun-shee)	允许
personal	*siren-de* (suh-wren-der)	私人的

pharmacy	*yaodian (yow-dee-an)* 药店	
phone call	*dian hua (dee-an hwah)* 电话	
photo copy	*fuyin (foo-een)* 复印	
physical exam	*ti jian (tee jee-an)* 体检	
picnic	*yecan (yeh-tsahn)* 野餐	
picture	*huar (hwah-urr)* 画	
pill	*yao pian (yee-ow-pee-an)* 药片	
ping-pong	*pingpangqiu (peeng-pahng-chee-oh)* 乒乓球	
platform (train)	*zhantai (jahn-tie)* 站台	
playground	*caochang (tsow-chahng)* 操场	
poached egg	*shuizhudan (shway-joo-dahn)* 水煮蛋	
poison	*duwu (doo-woo)* 毒物	
police	*jingcha (jeeng-chah)* 警察	
police station	*gongan ju (gohng-ahn-jwee)* 公安局	
pollution	*wuran (woo-rahn)* 污染	
pool	*chi (chr)* 池	
pork	*zhurou (joo-roe)* 猪肉	
postage	*youfei (you-fay)* 邮费	
postage stamp	*youpiao (you-pee-ow)* 邮票	
post office	*you ju (you jwee)* 邮局	
present (gift)	*liwu (lee-woo)* 礼物	
priest	*mushi (moo-shr)* 牧师	
prescription	*yaofang (yow-fahng)* 药方	
present (gift)	*liwu (lee-woo)* 礼物	
president (company)	*zongcai (zohng-tsigh)* 总裁	
president (nation)	*zongtong (zohng-tohng)* 总统	
primary school	*xiao xue (she-ow shu-eh)* 小学	
printed matter	*yinshua pin (een-shwah peen)* 印刷品	
private	*siren (suh-wren)* 私人	
problem	*wenti (wern-tee)* 问题	
profession	*zhiye (jr-yeh)* 职业	
professional	*zhuanye (jwahn-yeh)* 专业	

pronunication   *fayin (fah-een)* 发音
property   *caichan (tsigh-chahn)* 财产
province   *sheng (sherng)* 省
public square   *guang chang (gwahng chahng)* 广场

[Q]
quality   *zhiliang (jr-lee-ahng)* 质量
quantity   *shuliang (shoo-lee-ahng)* 数量
question   *wenti (wern-tee)* 问题
queue   *paidui (pie-dway)* 排队
quiet, peaceful   *anjing (ahn-jeeng)* 安静

[R]
race (human)   *zhongzu (johng-joo)* 种族
radio   *shouyinji (show-een-jee)* 收音机
railway   *tielu (tee-eh-loo)* 铁路
railway station   *huoche zhan (hwoh-cher jahn)* 火车站
rain   *yushui (yuu-shway)* 雨水
raincoat   *yuyi (yuu-ee)* 雨衣
rainstorm   *baofengyu (bow-ferng-yuu)* 暴风雨
rate / price   *jiage (jee-ah-guh)* 价格
raw   *sheng-de (sherng-der)* 生的
razor blades   *tidao pian (tee-dow pee-an)* 剃刀片
ready   *hao-le (how-ler)* 好了
reception (party)   *zhaodaihui (jow-die-hway)* 招待会
reception desk   *fuwutai (foo-woo-tie)* 服务台
receptionist   *jiedaiyuan (jee-eh-die-ywen)* 接待员
refund   *tuikuan (tway-kwahn)* 退款
registered mail   *guahaoxin (gwah-how sheen)* 挂号信
regulation   *guilu (gway-lwee)* 规律
relationship /   *guanxi (gwahn-she)* 关系
   connection
relative, kin   *qinqi (cheen-chee)* 亲戚

religion	*zongjiao (zohng-jee-ow)* 宗教	
rent, hire	*zu (joo)* 租	
reservation	*yuding (yuu-deeng)* 预定	
reservation desk	*yuding chu (yuu-deeng choo)* 预定处	
rest	*xiuxi (she-o-she)* 休息	
restaurant	*fanguan (fahn-gwahn)* 饭馆	
return ticket	*laihui piao (lie-hway pee-ow)* 来回票	
reverse charges	*duifangfufei (dway-fahng-foo-fay)* 对方付费	
rice (cooked)	*baifan (by-fahn)* 白饭	
rice (uncooked)	*mi (me)* 米	
ring (jewelry)	*jiezhi (jee-eh-jr)* 戒指	
river	*he (her)* 河	
road	*lu (loo)* 路	
romanization	*luomahua (lwoh-mah-hwah)* 罗马化	
room	*fangjian (fahng-jee-an)* 房间	
room number	*fangjian haoma (fahng-jee-an how-mah)* 房间号码	
round-trip	*laihui (lie-hway)* 来回	
round-trip ticket	*laihui piao (lie-hway pee-ow)* 来回票	
row, line, queue	*pai (pie)* 排	

[S]

sack, bag	*koudai (koe-die)* 口袋	
safe (noun)	*baoxianxiang (bow-she-an-shee-ahng)* 保险箱	
sales manager	*xiaoshou jingli (she-ow-show jeeng-lee)* 销售经理	
sales person	*dianyuan (dee-an ywahn)* 店员	
sales tax	*yingye shui (eeng-yeh shway)* 营业税	
sample	*yangping (yahng-peeng)* 样品	
sandwich	*sanmingzhi (sahn-meeng-jr)* 三明治	
San Francisco	*Jiujin Shan (Jeo-jeen shahn)* 旧金山	

sanitary towel	*weishengjing (way-sherng-jeeng)*	卫生巾
scenery	*fengjing (ferng-jeeng)*	风景
schedule	*richengbiao (rr-churng-bee-ow)*	日程表
scholar	*xuezhe (shu-eh-juh)*	学者
scrambled eggs	*chao jidan (chow jee-dahn)*	炒鸡蛋
seashore, beach	*haitan (high-tahn)*	海滩
seasick	*yunchuan (ywun-chwahn)*	晕船
seat	*zuowei (zwoh-way)*	座位
seatbelt	*anquan dai (ahn-chwahn die)*	安全带
secretary	*mishu (me-shoo)*	秘书
security guard	*anquan renyuan (ahn-chwahn wren-ywahn)*	安全人员
seminar	*yantaohui (yahn-tou-hway)*	研讨会
Seoul, Korea	*Hancheng (Hahn-churng)*	汉城
serious (injury)	*yanzhong (yahn-johng)*	严重
service attendant	*fuwu yuan (foo-woo ywah)*	服务员
service desk	*fuwu tai (foo-woo tie)*	服务台
service fee	*fuwu fei (foo-woo fay)*	服务费
sex	*xing (sheeng)*	性
shake hands	*wo shou (woh show)*	握手
ship	*haichuan (high-chwahn)*	海船
sightseeing	*youlan (you-lahn)*	游览
signature	*qianming (chee-in-meeng)*	签名
silk	*sichou (suh-choe)*	丝绸
Silk Road	*Sichou Zhi Lu (Suh-choe Jr Loo)* 丝绸之路	
single, unmarried	*danshen (dahn-shern)*	单身
single room	*danjian (dahn-jee-an)*	单间
sitting room	*keting (ker-teeng)*	客厅
size	*daxiao (dah-shee-ow)*	大小
size (clothes)	*chicun (chr-tswun)*	尺寸
sleeping berth	*wo pu (woh poo)*	卧铺
sleeping car	*wo che (woh cher)*	卧车

snack	*xiaochi (shee-ow-chr)*	小吃
socket (electric)	*chazuo (chah-zwoh)*	插座
soda water	*qi shui (chee shway)*	汽水
soft drink	*qingliang yinliao (cheeng-lee-ahng een-lee-ow)*	清凉饮料
souvenir	*jinianpin (jee-nee-an-peen)*	纪念品
soy sauce	*jiang you (jee-ahng you)*	酱油
spicy	*la (lah)*	辣
sports	*yundong (ywun-dohng)*	运动
square (place)	*guangchang (gwahng-chahng)*	广场
stadium	*tiyuchang (tee-yuu-chahng)*	体育场
station	*zhan (jahn)*	站
stationery	*wenju (wern-jwee)*	文具
stationery store	*wenju dian (wern-jwee dee-an)*	文具店
straight ahead	*yizhi (ee-jr)*	一直
street	*jie (jee-eh)*	街
student	*xuesheng (shu-eh-sherng)*	学生
suburbs	*jiaoqu (jee-ow-chwee)*	郊区
subway station	*ditie chezhan (dee-tee-eh cher-jahn)*	地铁车站
suitcase	*xiangzi (she-ahng-dzu)*	箱子
suite	*yitao fangjian (ee-tou fahng-jee-an)*	一套房间
sunburn	*shaishang (shy-shahng)*	晒伤
sunglasses	*mojing (mwo-jeeng)*	墨镜
suntan lotion	*shaiheigao (shy-hay-gow)*	晒黑膏
Sun Yat-sen	*Sun Zhong-shan (Soon Johng-shahn)*	孙中山
supermarket	*chaojishichang (chow-jee-shr-chahng)*	超级市场
swimming pool	*youyong chi (you-yohng chr)*	游泳池
swimsuit	*youyong yi (you-yohng ee)*	游泳衣
switchboard	*zongji (zohng-jee)*	总机

swollen	*zhong-le (johng-ler)*	肿了
symphony	*jiaoxiangyue (jee-ow-shee-ahng-yuu-eh)*	
	交响乐	

[T]

talks, meetings	*huitan (hway tahn)*	会谈
taste, flavor	*wei (way)*	味
tasty	*haochi (how-chr)*	好吃
tax free	*mian shui (mee-an shway)*	免税
telephone	*dianhua (dee-an-hwah)*	电话
technology	*jishu (jee-shoo)*	技术
television	*dianshi (dee-an-shr)*	电视
temperature	*wendu (wern-doo)*	温度;
body	*tiwen (tee-wern)*	体温;
weather	*qiwen (chee-wern)*	气温;
Centigrade	*sheshi (she-shr)*	摄氏
Fahrenheit	*huashi (hwah-shr)*	华氏
temple	*siyuan (suh-ywahn)*	寺院
tennis	*wangqiu (wahng-cheo)*	网球
tennis court	*wangqiu chang (wahng-cheo chahng)*	
	网球场	
theater	*juchang (jwee-chahng)*	剧场
theater ticket	*xipiao (shee-pee-ow)*	戏票
thermometer	*wendubiao (wern-doo-bee-ow)*	温度表
thirsty	*kele (ker-ler)*	渴了
century egg	*pi dan (pee dahn)*	皮蛋
Tiananmen Square	*Tian An Men (Tee-an Ahn Mern)*	
	天安门	
tiger	*laohu (lao-hoo)*	老虎
tip (gratuity)	*xiaofei (she-ow-fay)*	小费
tissue paper	*mian zhi (mee-an jr)*	绵纸
toast (bread)	*kaomianbao (kow-mee-an-bow)*	
	烤面包	

toilet	*cesuo (tser-swoh)* 厕所	
toilet paper	*shou zhi (show jr)* 手纸	
Tokyo	*Dongjing (Dohng-jeeng)* 东京	
toothbrush	*yashua (yah-shwah)* 牙刷	
toothpaste	*yagao (yah-gow)* 牙膏	
toothpick	*yaqian (yah-chee-an)* 牙签	
torch (flashlight)	*shoudiantong (show-dee-an-tohng)* 手电筒	
tour	*luxing (lwee-sheeng)* 旅行	
tour escort	*lingdui (leeng-dway)* 领队	
tour group	*luxingtuan (lwee-sheeng-twahn)* 旅行团	
tournament	*bisai (bee-sigh)* 比赛	
traffic	*jiaotong (jee-ow-tohng)* 交通	
traffic circle	*jiaotong huandao (jee-ow-tohng hwahn-dow)* 交通换道	
traffic light	*hongludeng (hohng-lwee-derng)* 红绿灯	
train	*huoche (hwoh-cher)* 火车	
dining car	*can che (tsahn chuh)* 餐车	
express train	*te kuai (ter kwie)* 特快	
fast train	*kuai che (kwie cher)* 快车	
reclining car	*tang yi (tahng ee)* 躺椅	
sleeping car	*wo pu (woh poo)* 卧铺	
transfer (train or bus line)	*huan che (hwahn cher)* 换车	
translate	*fanyi (fahn-ee)* 翻译	
translator	*fanyi (fahn-ee)* 翻译员	
transportation	*yunshu (ywun-shoo)* 运输	
transportation charges	*yunshu feiyong (ywun-shoo fay-yohng)* 运输费用	
travel agency	*luxing she (lu-sheeng shuh)* 旅行社	
traveler's checks	*luxing zhipiao (lwee-sheeng jr-pee-ow)* 旅行支票	

treatment (medical)	*zhiliao (jr-lee-ow)*	治疗
typewriter	*daziji (dah-dzu-jee)*	打字机
typhoon	*taifeng (tie-ferng)*	台风

[U]

umbrella	*yusan (yuu-sahn)*	雨伞
uncomfortable	*bushufu (boo-shoo-foo)*	不舒服
underpass	*dixia guodao (dee-shee-ah gwoh-dow)*	底下过道
uniform	*zhifu (jr-foo)*	制服
United States	*Mei Guo (May Gwoh)*	美国
universal	*pubian (poo-bee-an)*	普遍
university	*daxue (dah-shu-eh)*	大学
urgent matter	*jishi (jee-shr)*	急事
urinate	*xiaobian (shee-ow-bee-an)*	小便
urine	*niao (nee-ow)*	尿

[V]

vacancy	*kongfangjian (kohng-fahng-jee-an)*	空房间
vacation	*fangjia (fahng-jee-ah)*	放假
vaccination	*fangyi (fahng-ee)*	防疫
valuable	*zhengui (jern-gway)*	珍贵
vegetarian	*chisu-de (chee-soo-der)*	吃素的
veneral disease	*xingbing (sheeng-beeng)*	性病
video camera	*luxiang ji (loo-shee-ang jee)*	录象机
Vietnam	*Yuenan (Yuu-eh-nahn)*	越南
village	*cunzhuang (tswun-jwahng)*	村庄
visa	*qianzheng (chee-an jerng)*	签证
visitor, guest	*keren (ker-wren)*	客人
vocabulary	*cihui (tsu-hway)*	词汇
vodka	*futejia (foo-ter-jee-ah)*	伏特加
volleyball	*paiqiu (pie-cheo)*	排球

voltage	*dianya (dee-an-yah)*	电压
vomit	*outu (oh-too)*	呕吐

[W]

wait	*deng (derng)*	等
waiter, waitress	*fuwuyuan (foo-woo-ywahn)*	服务员
waiting room	*houke shi (hoe-ker shr)*	候客室
walk (noun)	*sanbu (sahn-boo)*	散步
wallet	*pijiazi (pee-jee-ah-dzu)*	皮夹子
wall poster	*guanggao hua (gwahng-gow-hwah)* 广告画	
warm	*nuanhuo (nwahn-hwoh)*	暖和
wash, clean	*xi (she)*	洗
washing machine	*xiyi ji (she-ee jee)*	洗衣机
watch (wrist)	*shou biao (show-bee-ow)*	手表
water	*shui (shway)*	水
waterfront	*haibin (high-bin)*	海滨
way, lane	*lu (loo)*	路
weather	*tianqi (tee-an-chee)*	天气
weather forecast	*tianqi yubao (tee-an-chee yuu-bow)* 天气预报	
wedding	*hunli (hoon-lee)*	婚礼
weekend	*zhoumo (joe-mwo)*	周末
welcome	*huanying (hwahn-eeng)*	欢迎
Westernized	*Xihua-de (She-hwah-duh)*	西化的
Western toilet	*zuoshi cesuo (zwoh-shr tser-swoh)* 坐式厕所	
windbreaker	*fengyi (ferng-ee)*	风衣
wine	*putaojiu (poo-tao-jeo)*	葡萄酒
wine pub	*jiuba (jeo-bah)*	酒吧
winter	*dongtian (dohng-tee-an)*	冬天
wound	*dashang (dah-shahng)*	打伤
wrap	*baozhuang (bow-jwahng)*	包装

wristwatch	*shoubiao (show-bee-ow)* 手表
write	*xie (she-eh)* 写
writing paper	*xinshi (sheen-jr)* 信纸
written language	*wen zi (wern dzu)* 文字
wrong	*cuo-le (tswoh-ker)* 错了

[X]

| x-ray | *x-guangpianzi (x-gwahng-pee-an-dzu)* X-光片子 |

[Y]

Yangtse River	*Chang Jiang (Chahng Jee-ahng)* 长江
year	*nian (nee-an)* 年
yearly	*niannian (nee-an-nee-an)* 年年
yellow	*huangse (hwahng-suh)* 黄色
Yellow River	*Huang He (Hwahng Her)* 黄河
yesterday	*zuotian (zwoh-tee-an)* 昨天
yogurt	*suanniunai (swahn-new-nigh)* 酸牛奶
your	*ni-de (nee-der)* 你的

[Z]

zero	*ling (leeng)* 零
zipper	*lalian (lah-lee-an)* 拉链
zoo	*dongwuyuan (dohng-woo-ywahn)* 动物园